RAILWAY · TIMES ·

Contents

The · Transport · Treasury

TIMES SERIES

Front Cover: With an audience of official lineside spectators, Class A4 No. 60034 *Lord Faringdon* makes a spirited departure from King's Cross emitting a volcanic exhaust as it does so at 1:10pm on Tuesday 20 April 1948 on its first test run to Leeds at the commencement of the Locomotive exchange trials. Pre-test runs for each trial were scheduled for Mondays and Wednesdays for down trains and Tuesdays and Thursdays for up trains with actual test runs, complete with dynamometer car which can be seen behind the tender in this view, scheduled for the following days. The pre-test run from King's Cross on the previous day, Monday 19 April, had been hauled by Royal Scot Class No. 46162. (See article on the Locomotive exchange trials on page 15 and reference to the change of name for *Lord Faringdon* in the article Nameplate News on page 66.)

Above: Newly renumbered No. 34022 *Exmoor* and No. 34064 *Fighter Command* on shed at Eastleigh with 'British Railways' now emblazoned on the tenders. Renumbering from 21C122 to 34022 took place on 12 June 1948 and renumbering from 21C164 to 34064 took place on 3 June 1948. The last of the pacifics released to traffic with a number in Bulleid's strange notation was 21C170 Manston which entered service on 21 October 1947. Thereafter the new BR numbering system was applied to No. 34071 601 *Squadron* onwards, this locomotive entering traffic in April 1948. Also in view are a newly out-shopped Z and a T9. To the right is the preserved Adams T3 4-4-0 No. 563.
IMAGE SOURCE: S C TOWNROE

Rear cover: Testing temporary bridge No. 126 situated on the East Coast Main Line (ECML) between Grantshouse and Reston. The test took place using Class D49 No. 62706 *Forfarshire* and Class A4 No. 60012 *Commonwealth of Australia* on 21 October 1948, just ten weeks after catastrophic floods in August severed the main line in multiple places and destroyed or damaged a considerable number of bridges. The steam boiler in the foreground was used to power the pile drivers. Re-opening the line to passenger traffic on 1 November was a remarkable achievement given the scale of the destruction which is particularly evident in this view. **IMAGE SOURCE: LORNE ANTON, AYTON LOCAL HISTORY SOCIETY**

Copies of images used within RAILWAY TIMES and sourced from the Transport Treasury archive are available for purchase/download. Please quote the Issue, article, page number, and if shown the reference.

In addition the Transport Treasury Archive contains tens of thousands of other UK, Irish and some European railway photographs.

© Images and design: The Transport Treasury 2023

ISBN 978-1-913251-46-8

First Published in 2023 by Transport Treasury Publishing Ltd.
16 Highworth Close, High Wycombe, HP13 7PJ

Compiled and designed in the UK. Printed in Tarxien, Malta by Gutenberg Press Ltd.

www.ttpublishing.co.uk *or for editorial issues and contributions email* **admin@ttpublishing.com**

INTRODUCTION

Having successfully launched three previous titles in the expanding 'Times' series of publications, namely 'Southern Times', 'Western Times' and 'Midland Times' and with plans to extend the range further Transport Treasury are pleased to announce the arrival of this new periodical 'Railway Times'. The aim is to cover one year in the life of British Railways (BR) with each magazine on a biannual basis appearing in March and September each year. 2023 is the 75th anniversary year of nationalisation of the railways so we begin logically enough with 1948, a time of great change when the four railway companies formed at the Grouping twenty-five years previously were merged into the nationally owned BR comprising initially six geographical regions – Southern, Western, London Midland, Eastern, North Eastern and Scottish.

It is the intention to highlight in words and images for all BR regions not only the important events of each year but some of the quirkier occurrences that the elapse of three quarters of a century has made even more fascinating. In this first issue we naturally enough begin with the big story of the year - nationalisation, which was effective from 1 January 1948, outlining the new organisation and the visible manifestations of the new order from timetables and signage to liveries and numbering. The other major story of 1948 was the disastrous floods which occurred during August in the Scottish Borders, closing the East Coast Main Line (ECML) for almost 3 months.

In a year full of momentous events, other topics included in this issue cover the locomotive exchange trials, the introduction of new locomotives, which still continued to roll off the production lines in some numbers, and the sad exit of the last examples of some of the old stagers. Coaches and infrastructure are not overlooked and of course line closures, not just a feature of the later Beeching era, are also covered. Although colour photography of railways was not common at that time, such images as are available have been used to illustrate the various liveries and markings of the new railway. Named expresses, both old favourites and new brands, always make the news and views of some of these can be found within. Most of the images have been sourced from the vast Transport Treasury archive but I would like to record my special thanks to the local history society based in the village of Ayton in the former county of Berwickshire who have provided some stunning views of the impact of the floods on the railways of the area in August 1948 together with views of some of the work of reconstruction which it is hoped to feature in subsequent issues.

We are always open to constructive comments from readers and feedback upon the items covered would also be welcomed. I must apologise in advance if I have omitted something that you felt should have been featured during 1948 but to cover a whole year's worth of events in just 80 pages is something of a tall order. It was felt preferable to cover as many subjects as possible rather than concentrate upon just a handful of topics. Contributions both in terms of articles and images are invited and fees will be paid for any used in future editions. For the next issue covering the year 1949, due to be published in September 2023, it is planned to include SR double deck EMUs, the Liverpool Street - Shenfield electrification and a look at the ill-fated Tavern Cars along with the retirement of Oliver Bulleid, their controversial designer.

My own railway memories do not stretch back quite as far as 1948 but I do recall being taken, courtesy of a child's seat fixed to the crossbar of my father's bicycle (Health & Safety look away now!), to see the passage of what we called the "Three Ms", the Midlander, Mancunian and Merseyside expresses during the early 1950s as they thundered through a cutting near Bletchley where we were living at the time. Hopefully we may feature images of some of these named trains in future volumes but in the meantime welcome to this inaugural issue and I hope you find something of interest within its pages.

EDITOR: *JEFFERY GRAYER*

Nationalisation - the outward and visible manifestations of change

Under the nationalisation of the railways, rolling stock received new colours and new logos. This process is shown being applied at Derby shed to Jubilee Class No. 45565 *Victoria* in an image taken on 25 May 1948. One of the first visible signs of change was the painting of BRITISH RAILWAYS on the tanks and tenders of locomotives, replacing the former Big Four company names. Following much discussion and feedback from the general public in 1948, it was not until the following year that BR formally issued details of their chosen standard liveries. One aspect of this corporate branding was the new BR emblem which came to be universally known as the 'Cycling Lion' which I suppose was slightly better than the epithet awarded to its replacement, which came along in 1956, derided as the 'Ferret and Dartboard' although there is some evidence in the railway press that this soubriquet applied to the later logo had in fact originated with the 1948 design. Conveniently the logo could be reversed so that the lion always faced forwards on a locomotive tender and one of the first locomotives to receive the lion emblem was Hall Class No. 6910 *Gossington Hall* in the summer of 1948. IMAGE SOURCE: TOP LEFT: MEDIADRUM IMAGE. TOP RIGHT: TRANSPORT TREASURY.

Nationalisation is a vast subject which we cannot hope to cover fully in the limited space available here so certain of the more visible aspects of the new ownership have been chosen.

REGIONAL ORGANISATION

In an echo of the famous 'Five Boys' Fry's chocolate advertisement, the history of the railways in the UK from 1948 stretching back over the last 150 years can perhaps be summed up as 'Separation – Amalgamation – Unification' with 123 different railway companies coming together at the 1923 grouping to form the "Big Four" which now, twenty-five years later, had been combined into a unified whole as 'British Railways'. To present a new unified organisation to both railwaymen and the public, new national symbols were introduced and the various stock numbering systems then in operation were clarified. The four main line railway companies, together with the various joint lines and minor railways which had been under government control since 1939, passed into

the ownership of the British Transport Commission (BTC). The Railway Executive would be responsible for the day to day running and management of British Railways and the organisation was split into six regions which in summary were as follows –

To give a separate identity to the new organisation as soon as possible, the Railway Executive's advertising officer A. J. White created what would come to be the much loved and in later years much collected elongated totem shape which was used for station name signs with a background of the regional colour. Whilst being perfectly acceptable on stations, documents, publicity and advertising material, the totem shape looked hideous when applied to locomotives as witness the atrocity perpetrated upon the tender of Schools Class No. 926 Repton at Brighton Works in March 1948 when a grossly enlarged totem stretching over half the width of the tender was applied. D.W. Winkworth in his book on the Schools class puts it thus – '.....926 had its tender repainted in differing styles, one each side, of the British Railways 'sausages'

REGION	HQ	ROUTE MILES	REGIONAL COLOUR
London Midland	Euston	4,993	Maroon
Western	Paddington	3,782	Chocolate brown
Southern	Waterloo	3,730	Dark green
Eastern	Liverpool Street	2,836	Dark blue
North Eastern	York	2,250	Tangerine
Scottish	Glasgow	1,823	Light blue and white *

* Reflecting the colours of the Scottish saltire cross

type totem or logo and went up to Waterloo still in malachite green for the result to be judged by railway officers. Mercifully the rolling stock was not inflicted with the monstrosity.' Staff magazines which had been previously published by each of the Big Four were now absorbed and published as regional variants of a new BR magazine, the first issue of which contained a lead article entitled 'A Fresh Start – A change in name but still the same 'Pride in the Job' and a message from the Chairman of the Railway Executive.

Joint lines and minor railways were to be assigned to the most appropriate geographical region, for example the Mersey Railway would become part of the London Midland region whilst the Kent & East Sussex Light Railway would become part of the Southern region. There were some subsequent boundary adjustments made later in the year, for example the dividing line between the Scottish and London Midland regions was redrawn immediately south of Gretna and the branches from Hexham to Saughtree, Reedsmouth to Morpeth and the Rothbury branch were transferred to the North Eastern region. *(Ed: In 1967 the North Eastern region would disappear as a separate entity and be absorbed into the Eastern region.)* In June 1948 the Carlisle to Silloth branch, which had previously been part of the Scottish area of the LNER, was transferred from the North Eastern to the London Midland region. In November the Railway Executive announced that there would be an extensive programme of route, station and goods depot re-adjustment in an effort to simplify supervision, reduce administrative costs and avoid duplication. The lines involved were generally those that crossed from one region to another, usually stemming from past competitive penetrations. Examples of such route transfers were the former LMS lines in South and Central Wales now passed from the Midland to the Western region and

the Newbury to Winchester line now passed from the Western to the Southern region. Other facilities transferring included Carlisle Canal locomotive depot from the Scottish to the London Midland region and the formerly joint stations of Penrith and Tebay now allocated solely to the London Midland region.

LIVERIES

On 30 January 1948 an exhibition was held at Kensington Olympia station, originally named Addison Road, to help the BTC and the Railway Executive decide upon the various liveries to be applied to its locomotives and stock. Locomotives sported plain black and a variety of shades of green, Black 5 No. M4762 for example being in malachite green, although the SR electric locomotive exhibited was finished in blue. Coaching stock was decked out in both a chocolate and cream reminiscent of former GWR colours and a crimson lake akin to pre-grouping Midland railway colours whilst an SR electric multiple unit set was in malachite green. There was a further exhibition held at Marylebone which included an A4 in what was described as a 'gaudy shade of blue', a B17 in LNER green with yellow lining, and a Class 5 4-6-0 in LNWR black with red white and grey lining. In addition there was an LMS coaching set on view finished with brown lower and light slate grey upper panels and an LMS suburban set in a lighter shade of red than usual plus two GWR corridor coaches in chocolate and cream.

In the summer following these public displays some fourteen trains, including the 'Royal Scot' and the 'Cornish Riviera Limited', were painted in various colours and operated in regular service around the country on both main and cross country routes which included King's Cross to Edinburgh, St. Pancras to Bradford, Bournemouth West to Waterloo and Glasgow to Aberdeen. The public were invited to comment although it was stated at the time that regional colours for rolling stock would not be practicable as it was the intention to make the greatest use of exchange of rolling stock throughout the regions in the interests of efficient utilisation. It had been provisionally decided to paint main line express locomotives in one or two shades of blue with a lining of red, cream and grey; lesser passenger locomotives in green with similar lining colours; and freight engines in black, again with similar lining colours. Coaching stock on steam hauled corridor trains would be either chocolate and cream, lined with black and golden yellow, or plum and spilt milk lined with bands of yellow-maroon-yellow separated by lines of spilt milk. Electric stock, both multiple units and locomotives, would be green and local suburban coaching stock maroon lined with golden yellow-black-golden yellow. The background colours of the new corporate totem station signs would also reflect the colour of the regions to which they applied.

Thus in 1948, with no clear policy yet decided individual railway works continued to paint rolling stock in their traditional liveries; the only indication of the new ownership was the substitution of 'BRITISH RAILWAYS' for former company titles on the sides of locomotive tanks and tenders. There continued to be variations in typeface used to display 'BRITISH RAILWAYS' with former Southern Railway classes utilising Bulleid's 'sunshine' lettering whilst Gill Sans could be seen on former LNER locomotives. Locomotives of the former LMS adopted a mixture of Gill Sans and bold Sans-serif whilst on former GWR types Egyptian style in metallic gold or yellow with red drop-shadow and black outlining was used. This mixture continued until the replacement of 'British Railways' with the lion and wheel emblem.

Mike King, author of several books on rolling stock, offers the following observations on the new liveries with specific reference to the Southern region – *Like everything BR in 1948, the newly-formed nationalised organisation was keen to establish a corporate image for their new venture. Carriage stock would feature large in this, but it was a little while before any tentative steps were taken in this direction. As far as the Southern region was concerned a visible change could be seen in June 1948, when two trains of vehicles appeared in different liveries – certainly very different from the various green colours employed since 1923.*

In that month, Bulleid coaching sets 299 and 788, plus three loose Maunsell vehicles, appeared in what has been described as "plum and spilt milk" livery – approximating to the old pre-Grouping LNWR colours, while Maunsell set 237 and three more loose Maunsell coaches were painted in the erstwhile GWR chocolate and cream livery. The former vehicles ran on the South Western section between Waterloo and Bournemouth/Weymouth, the latter on the South Eastern section between Ramsgate and Cannon Street. One has to ask why these liveries were chosen by the new BR management? The writer can only offer one suggestion – namely that as many of the express locomotives were going to be painted in the former GWR green livery and mixed traffic locos were to adopt the ex-LNWR black with red, cream and grey lining, perhaps these were seen to be complementary with those colours? Who knows? But despite this, some locomotives were repainted in a pale apple green to work with the sets of experimentally-painted stock. It all seemed like a bit of a mish-mash!

Whatever the choice, it seems that any idea of testing public reaction to them was either forgotten, or not pursued with any great enthusiasm, as ultimately, and after the public had had their say, neither livery was in fact selected for general use. The writer's father remembered seeing the "plum and spilt milk" set come under King Charles Road bridge at Surbiton soon after introduction and his reaction could hardly be described as favourable. Interestingly, this was the majority view and most SR-based members of the public who responded preferred malachite green! Time was to prove that the new colours were not very durable (rather like the BR express passenger locomotive blue livery) and observers were soon remarking on the over-ripening of the fruit and the considerable souring of the milk! Whether the chocolate and cream colours fared any better does not seem to have been recorded. However, both sets of coaches retained their "special finish" (as recorded on the carriage stock set record cards) until 1953/54.

Whatever the conclusions drawn from the public

In October 1948 Lord Nelson Class *Sir John Hawkins*, renumbered from 865 to 30865 in July, gets away from Eastleigh with a Bournemouth service comprising Bulleid set No. 788 which had been painted in the experimental BR "plum and spilt milk" livery. IMAGE SOURCE: COLOURAIL

consultation might have been (if any?), from April 1949 corridor coaches began to appear in what was officially described as crimson lake and cream colours with non-corridors in lined crimson lake. Passenger-rated vans might appear in either livery, depending on whether they were gangwayed or not – but in practice there was no hard and fast rule here since some corridor-equipped vans did appear in lined or plain crimson. Horseboxes and the like also appeared in plain crimson colours. The crimson shade has long been described as carmine red – never an official description despite its common usage – but crimson it most certainly was not – certainly not when compared to the old LMS crimson lake, being much redder and lacking the same depth of hue. To many the livery became known as "blood and custard" and, to the writer, this sums it up very well. The red colour also varied from works to works and some vehicles looked almost orange, while the cream was usually a much paler colour than the former GWR

shade – which was always more cream than ivory. Go into your kitchen and look at the Bird's custard tin!

Lining was applied at the borders between the two colours – black and gold – or in the equivalent positions on crimson coaches but it soon became apparent that variable heights of windows and depths of panelling, never mind other constructional differences, would defeat a uniform approach, so compromises were soon made. On Southern corridor stock for example the upper crimson band was soon omitted (this was a particular problem on Maunsell high-window vehicles), while after about 1951, lining was also omitted from non-corridor stock. Numbering was applied in golden-yellow 4-inch Gill Sans medium figures – complete with black surrounds to each figure – near the left-hand end in the waist panel or just below windows, with an 'S' prefix. This was soon revised to the right-hand end, so as to be conveniently near the tare weight and dimension plates, which were mounted low down on the left-hand end of every ex-SR coach. This obviated the need to walk the length of the coach to record the details against the carriage number. Somebody practical must have suggested this improvement! As BR standard coaches began to appear – which might carry the same number as an older pre-nationalisation vehicle, the latter then began to receive an 'S' suffix as well e.g. S1234S.

However, there were plenty of locomotive hauled coaches plus the electric stock that were going to remain in malachite green livery for some time to come and, starting in January 1948, coaches began to be outshopped without the word "Southern" on the side panels and with the number prefixed 'S' but still at the eaves in otherwise Southern Railway style. There were still also some vehicles remaining carrying Maunsell olive green – albeit gradually degrading. A good clean down and a re-varnish (a process at which the Southern was most adept) preserved many such obsolete paint finishes for many years and so some coaches used only occasionally, for example ex-LSWR wooden-panelled corridors, never appeared in crimson lake and cream but worked out their mileages in re-varnished SR green (of whatever shade), gradually darkening as the depth and number of varnish coats increased. In due course these received BR Gill Sans numbering and other lettering below the waistline so, in a black and white photograph, would be indistinguishable from a coach repainted in Southern region post-1956 green colours.

Whilst beyond the remit of this short review, a glance forward from 1956 is perhaps in order. The Southern region management were never taken with "blood and custard" and soon found the task of keeping the livery (particularly the cream panels) clean in smoke-laden 1950s Britain difficult, so when BR announced increased freedom and devolvement for the regions in 1955 they were quick to return to green livery.

(Ed: In 1949 BR formally announced its decisions upon standard liveries for coaching stock, opting for crimson lake with cream panels for main line corridor coaches and plain crimson lake for local steam services and passenger train vans. More details of these liveries together with those specified for locomotives will be given in the next volume of 'Railway Times' covering the year 1949.)

NUMBERING

Numbering of locomotives was regularised to reduce the confusion arising between locomotives of former railways which bore the same number and it separated motive power into steam, diesel, electric and gas turbine groups. The former LMS practice of showing a locomotive's number on the front of a steam locomotive was adopted with the use of a cast iron plate affixed to the smokebox door. As the numbering of ex-GWR locomotives remained unchanged their brass number plates remained in situ. In summary renumbering was as follows -

Western: Nos. 1-9999 for steam stock. Diesel electric shunters under construction will be numbered from 15100 and gas turbines 18000 and 18001.

Southern: Nos. 30000-39999 for steam stock with the exception of the Q1 Class which will be numbered from 33000, the West Country/Battle of Britain Class from 34000 and the Merchant Navy Class from 35000. Isle of Wight steam stock numbering will remain unchanged. Diesel electric shunters will be numbered from 15200 and diesel mechanical from 11000. Diesel electric main line locomotives will be numbered from 10200. Main line electric locomotives will be numbered from 20000.

London Midland: Nos. 40000-59999 for steam stock except those locomotives already numbered above 20000 which will be renumbered from 58000. Scottish steam locomotives of LMS origin will have 40000 added to their number. 1,600hp main line diesel electrics will be numbered from 10000, the 1,600hp diesel mechanical units from 10100, the 800hp diesel electrics from 10800 and the 350hp shunters from 12000.

Eastern and North Eastern steam locomotives will have 60000 added to their existing numbers and the unique 4-6-4 No. 10000 will be renumbered. Diesel shunters will be numbered from 15000 and electric locomotives from 26000.

No. 21C158 *Sir Frederick Pile* was the first SR locomotive to have the BR lettering on its tender and its number prefixed with an 's'. These alterations were made at Brighton Works in January 1948 and on the 18 January the engine was sent to Waterloo for official inspection of the result.

Diesel, Petrol and Gas Turbine locomotives will be numbered from 10000-19999.

Electric locomotives will be numbered from 20000-29999.

Standard types of steam locomotive planned for the future will be numbered from 70000 onwards.

Coaching stock from the Big Four companies will retain their old numbers but with a suffix W, S, M or E respectively for stock of GWR, SR, LMS or LNER origin. As there had been no separate Scottish company between 1923 and 1948, there were no specific locomotives to be renumbered as before former LMS and LNER locomotives provided the motive power on the Scottish region.

TRANSPORT ACT 1947

GREAT WESTERN RAILWAY COMPANY
LONDON MIDLAND & SCOTTISH RAILWAY COMPANY
LONDON & NORTH EASTERN RAILWAY COMPANY
SOUTHERN RAILWAY COMPANY
LONDON PASSENGER TRANSPORT BOARD

Notice is hereby given that in pursuance of the above Act the Undertakings of the above named bodies vest in the British Transport Commission on 1st January, 1948, and that on and after the said date all Byelaws, Regulations and Notices published by any of the said bodies and in operation immediately before the said date and all tickets, consignment notes and other documents issued or used on and after the said date and which bear the name of any of the said bodies shall be deemed to be published and issued by and in the name of the Railway Executive or the London Transport Executive (as the case may be) constituted under the said Act.

BY ORDER

31st December, 1947

Below: Looking resplendent in its new livery, Class J69 0-6-0T No. E8619 poses at Stratford in January 1948. This was the first locomotive to be painted in the new style with British Railways and the E prefix to the number in yellow, and to mark the occasion this locomotive was painted green and was to be later seen at Liverpool Street acting as station pilot. IMAGE SOURCE: REV 33B-5-3

Opposite Top: The Jensen Jen tug announced in 1947 as a "horse substitute vehicle" was a rather bizarre contraption purchased by BR in the early days of nationalisation. They were built in West Bromwich using a Ford side valve 1,172cc engine producing 30hp with column change gearbox and forward opening doors. It was a four wheel articulated "mechanical horse" with a very narrow rear wheelbase ideal for the diminishing loads then being carried by BR, having only a 30cwt limit. They were of lightweight construction with an alloy cab based on car components and hence had a rather short life span in the daily rough and tumble of BR use. An electric version called the Jen Helec was introduced in 1948. The first Jen tug for BR was delivered in February 1948 to Marylebone and was later transferred to Manchester Deanside. A later example was fitted with an Austin A40 engine and in addition to flat bed trailers some dozen or more different trailer types were offered including a large volume pantechnicon. Some 700 cab units and 1,400 trailers were manufactured during the model's lifetime. The Jen tug was a world away from the grand touring car, the Interceptor, that the Jensen firm later produced. Cab unit GG2301 with trailer GT1 are seen here watched over by a BR employee clad in a leather apron and with the typical 'fag on the go'. IMAGE SOURCE: REV 32B-6-2

Opposite Bottom: Paddington in 1948, the logo on a road wagon of private rail firm Great Western Railway (GWR) is spray-painted. IMAGE SOURCE: MEDIADRUM

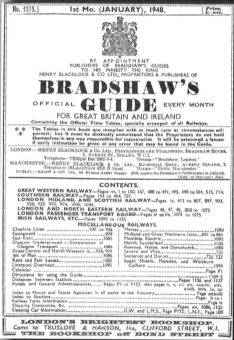

Top: The old order ... 1947.

Right: : Bradshaw's Guide for January 1948 - not quite keeping up with the changing times as the "Big Four" company names are still used throughout and, as the front page illustrated indicates, a number of what it calls "Miscellaneous" lines and joint lines such the Great Central and North Western Joint, the Somerset & Dorset Joint, Midland & Great Northern Joint as well as the soon to be closed Easingwold and East Kent railways. For February's issue however they did adopt the new regional titles at the head of each timetable page but still referred to the old titles in the contents and index as well continuing with the former titles of miscellaneous companies and joint lines. A typical January 1948 Bradshaw's timetable page continues to show LMS at the top of the timetable covering services from Delph to Oldham and Leeds to Huddersfield via Heckmondwike (Spen).

Bottom: The new order.

The times they are a-changin'
'Come gather round people wherever you roam...'

The opening lyrics of the song made famous by Bob Dylan in 1964 are perhaps apposite for travellers of 1948 when the timetables of the "Big Four" were standardised under the new British Railways umbrella. Along with the famous Bradshaw's Guide and the ABC for Travellers Guide which continued in production for many years, the six regions of the newly created BR produced their own guides in the new regional colours.

Bradshaw's, whose travel guides are so beloved of Michael Portillo in his series of travel programmes, was part of a series of railway timetable and travel guide books published by W.J. Adams and later by Henry Blacklock. They were named after the founder, one George Bradshaw, who produced his first timetable in October 1839. The railway timetables were published monthly with the final edition rolling off the presses in May 1961.

The ABC Rail Guide, first published in 1853 as The ABC or Alphabetical Railway Guide, was also a monthly timetable guide but only showed times of trains to and from the capital to what it called "the principal stations of Britain" although it was organised on an alphabetical basis with the slogan "As easy as ABC" which some people felt made it easier to use than Bradshaw's which had something of a reputation for difficulty amongst the travelling public although it never seemed to confuse Sherlock Holmes or Dr. Watson who made frequent use of it in Conan Doyle's stories. Bradshaw's and The ABC Guide were just a couple of many railway timetable guides published during the great expansion of the British railway network in the Victorian era. For the January 1948 issue they did manage to adopt the new BR nomenclature except where differentiating between one station and another. After a number of changes of publisher in the later twentieth century, The ABC Guide was renamed the OAG Rail Guide in 1996, ceasing publication in 2007.

Getting back to British Railways, the last pre-nationalisation company timetables were produced for the winter service 1947-48 with the 1948 summer timetables commencing on 31 May 1948 being the first from the new BR regions. They were in the new regional colours and to a uniform format and size measuring 6½ ins. x 4½ ins. This meant a radical reduction in size for the Western region as the former GWR timetables had measured 11½ ins. x 7½ ins. No doubt the reduction in size was done to make them more manageable to handle for the public but this did of course mean less clarity as the size of the print was that much smaller. Of course the GWR, being the GWR, had continued to plough their own furrow as their timetable was the only one of the Big Four companies that had retained this larger format well into the 1940s. The Southern Railway had been the first to substitute reprints from Bradshaw into its own public timetables in 1924 whilst the LNER did this in May 1939 followed by the LMS in September of that year. Bradshaw reprints had been used before in wartime when, towards the end of World War I in 1917, the GWR and LNWR had used them in their staff timetables when public timetable production was under wartime suspension. Even in those days of uniformity in 1948 there were some variations, for example the Scottish region timetable cost 3d whereas the Southern region timetable was 6d, no doubt a reflection of the volume of entries, relating as it did to the frequency of services and complexity of routes of both region's timetables.

Rail privatisation during the 1990s didn't immediately affect printed timetable production, however, technological advances eventually hastened its demise as in December 2006 Network Rail made the timetable freely available on their website and by the following May the last printed edition appeared. With its size reduced to just 5¾ x 8¾ ins. and consequent reduction in print size, it contained a staggering 2,752 pages, albeit of very flimsy paper, and cost a whopping £12, covering a period of just 6 months. The reason for ceasing production of the national printed timetable at that point was given as the fact that 'demand has declined over recent years to the point where it is uneconomical to print'.

The 1948 locomotive exchange trials schedules

When the recently nationalised BR announced their intention of running locomotive trials during April-May 1948, which was in fact extended until the end of August, there was speculation about the reasoning behind it. Ostensibly the trials were undertaken as a means of obtaining information, from live running tests conducted out on the main lines of the newly formed regions, upon which to base plans for the most efficient standards of locomotive construction for the future. The adoption of best practice in design was the aim. We shall examine the results of the trial in the next edition of "Railway Times" for 1949 but even today opinion is still very much divided about the utility of such trials. Was it just a publicity stunt to advertise the new go - ahead British Railways? Was it done to appease the locomotive designers of the Big Four? Had Riddles & Co. already made up their minds about the design of the new Standard locomotives? Of course the trials had the added bonus of being a locospotter's and serious railway observer's dream, being able to see "foreign" locomotives in their home patch, but this was hardly the raison d'être for the trials.

In this issue we are concerned solely with the planned timetable of trials detailing the various locomotives used routes followed and parameters

Opposite: Royal Scot No. 46162 *Queen's Westminster Rifleman* leaves King's Cross with dynamometer car attached on a preliminary run on Thursday 29 April. This Scot had been rebuilt in January of that year as part of the programme that saw all class members so treated between 1943 and 1955. Although sporting its new BR number, it retained LMS on the tender. IMAGE SOURCE: REV 34A/5

Above: As smoke drifts lazily from the chimney, Merchant Navy No. 35019 *French Line CGT* attached to a former LMS tender waits near King's Cross York Road platform on 18 May 1948. IMAGE SOURCE: REV37/A/6/5

laid down for the tests. Beginning with the rules governing the trials, it was first of all decided that crews from the home regions should handle their own steeds on foreign metals, that the coal supplied should be of uniform quality throughout all the tests and that loads should be equalised generally up to the maximum load permitted for each class. On many of the routes chosen there were stiff banks to be climbed as well as "racing grounds" to show off a locomotive's paces. Due to restricted clearances some locomotives were not able to run on some routes, for example the

Kings were restricted to the route out of King's Cross whilst the Halls were barred from the Perth – Aberdeen and Manchester – Marylebone routes. Tenders would need to be fitted with water pick up apparatus in view of the non-stop distances involved on some of the longer runs, this applying particularly to SR types which were not so fitted and which in the event carried ex-LMS tenders. Three classes of locomotive would be tested – express passenger, mixed traffic and freight. Dynamometer cars would be included in the rakes hauled to record performance.

Above: Coronation Class No. 46236 *City of Bradford* with dynamometer car attached leaves King's Cross on 6 May 1948. IMAGE SOURCE: 37/B/1/3

Opposite: No. 35017 *Belgian Marine* enters Finsbury Park at a little after noon on 26 May 1948 passing the impressive signal gantry with the 07:50 service to King's Cross which it had hauled from Leeds. IMAGE SOURCE: JCF E7-3

EXPRESS PASSENGER LOCOMOTIVES

	LOCOMOTIVES KNOWN TO HAVE BEEN USED		
Duchess	46236		
A4	60034	60033	60022 *
Merchant Navy	35019	35017	35018
Royal Scot	46162	46154	
King	6018		

MIXED TRAFFIC

Black 5	45253	44973	
B1	61251	61292	61163
West Country	34006	34005	34004
Hall	6990		

FREIGHT

8F	48189	48400
O1	63773	63789
WD 2-8-0	63169	77000
WD 2-10-0	73774	73776
38XX	3803	

SERVICES/ROUTES

Express passenger

10am	Euston – Carlisle
12:55pm	Carlisle – Euston
7:50am	Leeds – King's Cross
1:10pm	King's Cross – Leeds
8:30am	Plymouth – Paddington
1:30pm	Paddington – Plymouth
10:50am	Waterloo – Exeter
12:40pm	Exeter – Waterloo

Mixed Traffic

8:40am	Inverness – Perth
4pm	Perth – Inverness
10:15am	St. Pancras – Manchester
1:50pm	Manchester – St. Pancras
1:45pm	Bristol – Plymouth
1:35pm	Plymouth – Bristol
10am	Marylebone – Manchester
9:55am	Manchester – Marylebone

Freight

Toton – Brent **
London – Peterborough
London – Severn Tunnel Junction
Bristol - Eastleigh

* Failed at Exeter

** 38XX did not operate this service

Attracting the customer: 1948 style

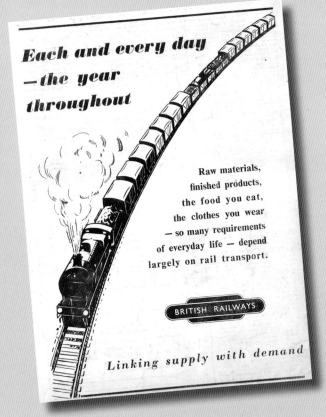

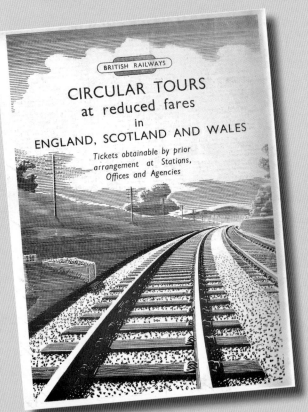

Peppercorn's new pacifics

You wait ages for a new pacific design and then two emerge within a few months of each other! Such was the case at the end of 1947 and early in 1948 when the former CME of the LNER, now of the Eastern and North Eastern regions of BR, Arthur Peppercorn, saw his A2 and A1 designs come to fruition.

A2

Following the retirement of the previous CME Edward Thompson, a decision was taken to modify his design for 15 locomotives which had already been ordered. These design modifications, whilst retaining Thompson's cylinder and valve arrangement, adopted a more conventional position for the outside cylinders, positioned as they now were between the bogie wheels which themselves had been brought back nearer the driving wheels thus resulting in a shortening of the total wheelbase. A rocking grate was also fitted. Although it was originally intended to fit a Kylchap exhaust, this was discarded as it would not have been practicable to retain it with the self-cleaning smokebox which was now shorter than that originally designed. Nickel alloy steel enabled thinner barrel plates to be used in the boiler and the cab had been widened with the lookout for crewmen being improved by alteration in the layout of some of the cab fittings. The size of the original order was increased from 15 to 35 units but in May 1948 the last 20 were cancelled pending the results of the BR Exchange Trials.

The first A2 emerged from Doncaster Works just before Christmas 1947 and was named at

A2 No. 60521 *Watling Street*, built at Doncaster in May 1947, is seen at Carlisle a year later with its BR lettering and number which was applied in May 1948. On the opposite side of the platform an unidentified tank locomotive still sports LMS on its tank sides. **IMAGE SOURCE: GEO55**

A1 No. 60114 *W. P. Allen* **arrives into King's Cross shortly after naming which took place in October 1948.** IMAGE SOURCE: NS206602

Marylebone in honour of the designer with the remainder being rather suitably named after racehorses. The attractive appearance of E525 was universally admired incorporating as it did many modern features such as the self-cleaning smokebox and a Stone turbo generator providing electric lighting. The single chimney originally fitted did cause some initial steaming problems but the subsequent fitting of a double Kylchap blastpipe to the final A2 No. 60539, which meant that the self-cleaning apparatus had to be discarded did meet with success and five more examples were so modified in 1949. This led to improved steaming and fuel economy. The power, endurance and haulage capacity stemmed largely from the very large 50 sq.ft. grate area with which the class were endowed ensuring that they were some of the last multi cylindered express passenger locomotives to remain in service with the last three examples not being withdrawn until June 1966. In

their first year of operation they were allocated to depots along the ECML from Peterborough to Edinburgh hauling such prestigious services as the 'Flying Scotsman', 'Aberdonian' and 'Queen of Scots Pullman' although it was not until the following year that they really came into their own when allocated to the demanding Edinburgh – Aberdeen route.

A1

The first A1, No. 60114, left Doncaster Works in August 1948 to be followed by 9 further examples before the end of the year. Similar to the rebuilt prototype *Great Northern* No. 60113 which had been introduced 3 years before in 1945 by Thompson as a rebuild of Class A10, this new A1 type used not the A4 boiler as fitted to 60113 but an A2 type which was employed in the interests of standardisation. Also exchangeable with the new A2s were the cylinders and other components with

Table 2 - A2s delivered
December 1947 - August 1948

	Renumbered	Name	To Traffic
E525	60525	A. H. PEPPERCORN	24.12.47
E526	60526	SUGAR PALM	9.1.48
E527	60527	SUN CHARIOT	31.1.48
E528	60528	TUDOR MINSTREL	21.2.48
E529	60529	PEARL DIVER	21.2.48
E530	60530	SAYAJIRAO	4.3.48
E531	60531	BAHRAM	12.3.48
	60532	BLUE PETER *	25.3.48
	60533	HAPPY KNIGHT	9.4.48
	60534	IRISH ELEGANCE	23.4.48
	60535	HORNET'S BEAUTY	5.5.48
	60536	TRIMBUSH	14.5.48
	60537	BACHELOR'S BUTTON	11.6.48
	60538	VELOCITY	18.6.48
	60539	BRONZINO	27.8.48

* Preserved

Table 2 - A1s delivered in 1948

Number	Name	To Traffic
60114	W. P. ALLEN	6.8.48
60115	MEG MERRILIES	3.9.48
60116	HAL O' THE WIND	8.10.48
60117	BOIS ROUSSEL	22.10.48
60118	ARCHIBALD STURROCK	12.11.48
60119	PATRICK STIRLING	26.11.48
60120	KITTIWAKE	10.12.48
60121	SILURIAN	22.12.48
60122	CURLEW	24.12.48

the outside pair of cylinders, like the A2s, positioned between the front bogie wheels. In the interests of ease of maintenance, the class was not streamlined like its A4 predecessors. The outside cylinders acted on the axle of the middle set of driving wheels with the inside cylinder acting on the leading coupled axle. The 10 in. diameter piston valves were driven by three sets of Walschaerts valve gear and a rocking grate and hopper ashpan were fitted. A double chimney, turbo generator to power the electric lighting and a Flaman speed recorder were other refinements fitted to this prototype. A further eight examples would be delivered in 1948 followed by 41 more by the end of 1949. None were preserved but as is well known a new build A1 was completed in 2008 taking the next number in the sequence, No. 60163, and named Tornado by the Prince of Wales in 2009 accompanied appropriately enough by Peppercorn's widow Dorothy Mather. Although it had been the original intention to provide streamlining to both these new pacifics, this proposal was dropped and smoke deflectors of the Eastern region type cut away to give improved access to the inside motion were added to the front end.

There would eventually be 50 members of Class A1 including the original Thompson designed pacific No. 60113 named Great Northern and classified A1/1.

A2 Class No. 60533 *Happy Knight* captured at Ponton in Lincolnshire on the ECML during 1948. IMAGE SOURCE: AF0935

Don't forget Issue 2 of RAILWAY TIMES featuring the BR year 1949. Available in the Autumn of 2023.

Straight outta Horwich!

One of the new classes of locomotive emerging during 1948 was the Class 4F 2-6-0, designed by George Ivatt ,CME of the former LMS and now of the London Midland region, being constructed at Horwich Works in Lancashire. Twenty new freight locomotives, Nos. M3000-3019, were being built to replace the older 4F 0-6-0 freight locomotives which were being progressively withdrawn from service. The opportunity was taken in the design to effect improvements in both riding quality, the older Fowler 0-6-0s being notoriously rough riding, through the provision of a leading pony truck and in facilitating servicing and maintenance, this being evidenced by the accessibility afforded by the high running plate and outside cylinders. It was hoped to avoid the high incidence of "hot boxes", more prevalent with the older inside cylindered 0-6-0s, by the use of outside cylinders. Other features of note were the rocking grate with a 23 sq. ft. area, self-emptying ashpan and a self-cleaning smokebox all incorporated to reduce servicing time at depots. Piston valves, Walschaerts valve gear, and a double exhaust all gave this new design a modern look which would reduce the time needed to access components that required regular inspection and maintenance. The high running plate attached to the boiler rather than to the frames by brackets, although perhaps not to everyone's aesthetic taste, and which would in future years lead to the class being somewhat unkindly dubbed 'flying pigs' or 'doodlebugs', did enable fitting staff to readily access items on the boiler top such as cocks and pipe joints when required. One commentator at the time wished that '...it might have been possible to avoid the frankly hideous external lines of both locomotive and tender'.

First of the class No. 3000 is seen with an unidentified working at Bletchley. IMAGE SOURCE: FH93

The tender, with a capacity of 4,000 gallons of water and 9 tons of coal, had water pick up apparatus fitted as standard and a cab backplate and roof was mounted to give adequate protection to footplate crews during adverse weather. Regulator and brake handles were located on both sides of the cab to assist when shunting. The locomotive's driving wheels were of 5 ft. 3 in. diameter with the leading pony truck wheels of 3ft. diameter. The two outside cylinders were 17½ in. diameter with a stroke of 26 in. with boiler pressure set at 225 lb/sq.in. The total weight of locomotive and tender was 99 tons 8 cwt. The first member of the class, which was delivered on 6 December 1947, carried the number 3000 with LMS on the tender, and after running trials at Derby during December was allocated to Crewe South shed on 1 January 1948. No. 3001 saw the light of day on the 12th of the month with 3002 following on the last day of the old year. A further five examples, Nos. 3003-7, emerged from Horwich in January and February 1948 and the class would go on to number 162 in total over the following years, 75 being constructed at Horwich, 50 at Doncaster and 37 at Darlington with the last, No. 43161, emerging in September 1952. They were reclassified as 4MT by BR and could be found on secondary passenger work as well as freight duties, being particularly associated with the Midland & Great Northern Joint line. The original (by now renumbered) 43000 lasted in service for almost 20 years before being withdrawn from Blyth North shed in August 1966. Of the six class members which saw BR service into 1968, one, No. 43106, has been preserved on the Severn Valley Railway where it has covered more than 120,000 miles during its 55 years in preservation.

This view of Class A2 No. E530 *Sayajirao* heading the 'Queen of Scots' Pullman service near Potters Bar was photographed at 11:50am on 18 September 1948. **IMAGE SOURCE: PP449**

Named expresses

The year 1948 saw the return of some old favourites and the introduction of new named trains.

RETURNING TRAINS

ROYAL SCOT – On 16 February the 10am express from London to Glasgow resumed its name of 'Royal Scot' and carried appropriate carriage roofboards and headboard. The inaugural runs were appropriately hauled by 6242 *City of Glasgow* and 6245 *City of London*.

QUEEN OF SCOTS – July 5 saw the reinstatement of this Pullman car service running from Glasgow Queen Street to Edinburgh, Leeds and King's Cross, with the inaugural up train being hauled by Class A3 No. 60109 *Hermit* and the down by No. 60107 *Royal Lancer* between King's Cross and Leeds, and with B1 No. 61328 working from Glasgow.

FLYING SCOTSMAN – Resumption of non-stop running between King's Cross and Edinburgh, last seen in 1939, in a time of 7 hours 50 minutes.

NEW TRAINS

SOUTH YORKSHIREMAN – Running via the former Great Central route since 31 May, leaving Bradford Exchange at 10am and returning from London Marylebone at 4:50pm. The inaugural up service was hauled by Black 5 M5101. B1s were also observed on this working.

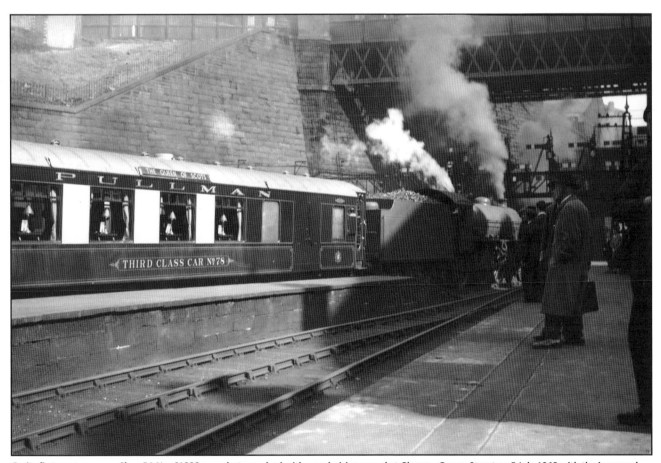

On its first post-war run, Class B1 No. 61328 was photographed with an admiring crowd at Glasgow Queen Street on 5 July 1948 with the inaugural 'Queen of Scots' Pullman service. **IMAGE SOURCE: WSA94**

This page: Using a Union Jack on a suspended wire, this is the unveiling of the inaugural 'South Yorkshireman' headboard attached to M5101 at Bradford Exchange on 31 May 1948. IMAGE SOURCE: G306

Opposite page: The brochure celebrating the 'Four Belles' of the Southern region. A separate brochure was produced for each of the four services with a different background colour giving information about the route. IMAGE SOURCE: BLUEBELL RAILWAY MUSEUM

THE NORFOLKMAN – Introduced with the winter timetable, the inaugural train of nine coaches was hauled by Class B1 No. 61000 *Springbok*, running from Liverpool Street to Ipswich and Norwich.

TEES-TYNE PULLMAN – This service ran each weekday between Newcastle, Darlington and King's Cross and allowed businessmen to reach the capital by 2:16pm and return again at 5:30pm and by contacting the Pullman conductor arrangements could be made for a car to be made available for the afternoon whilst in London. The inaugural up service was hauled by Class A1 No. 60115, later to be named *Meg Merrilies* in 1950.

THE THANET BELLE – With the commencement of the summer timetable on May 31, the Southern region launched a new summer only all Pullman service complementing their existing Pullman Car trains, the Devon, Bournemouth and Brighton Belle services. This new train, which served a number of resorts in Kent, was named the Thanet Belle. It is perhaps not strictly correct to call this train 'new' as back in 1921 the SE&CR inaugurated together with the Pullman Car Co., the "Thanet Pullman Limited", a Sunday only service

that could accommodate 124 passengers in first class surroundings. This service departed Victoria at 10:10 and called at Margate West, Broadstairs and Ramsgate Harbour, returning at 5:30pm with an arrival back in London at 7:15pm. Continued by the Southern for some time after the Grouping, the train was reduced to a mixed formation of Pullman and ordinary stock, being finally replaced by an express which included a Pullman car in 1931. A poster produced by the Southern region to celebrate the arrival of the new train was headed "The Four Belles Ring the Southern Coast" with four bells shown at the top and the names of the four trains radiating out from them, the 'Devon Belle' carrying the additional information 'Observation Car' and the "Thanet Belle" the suffix "New Train".

The new "Thanet Belle", which left Victoria seen off by the top hatted stationmaster Mr. Chapman, at the later time of 11:30am (SX) for Whitstable, Herne Bay, Margate, Broadstairs and Ramsgate, comprised two first class and eight third class Pullmans providing seats for 269 passengers in total. On Saturdays, as no timetabled path was available at 11:30am, an afternoon slot at 3:05pm was allocated. Travelling on the inaugural service in addition to railway dignitaries were six further "Belles" in the shape of the Beauty Queens crowned in the Kent County Beauty Competition for 1947 representing the five resorts and the county served by the new train. Members of the press and some of the staff from Brighton who had laboured on the coaches were also on the train that day. Normal Pullman supplements were applicable which at the time were 3/6 first class and 2/- third class. Bulleid pacifics were the normal motive power allocated in view of the weight of the train with its set of heavy Pullman cars and the exacting schedule to be observed the inaugural down run being headed suitably enough by 21C170 *Manston*, crewed by Driver White and Fireman Aird of Ramsgate depot who shared the footplate with Loco Inspector Hillman. This locomotive, whose name recognised the key role the Kentish airfield of that name had played in the Battle of Britain, had only been named at Ramsgate a couple of months previously.

It had originally been the intention of the Southern Railway to introduce the service in 1947 but due to lack of rolling stock, there being a shortage of some 500 coaches on the Southern Railway as no new stock had been constructed during the war according to Mr. R.M.T. Richards the Deputy Chief regional Officer, it had to be postponed until 1948. He paid tribute to the Pullman Car Company and workmen at Brighton who had laboured tirelessly to recondition and renovate the set of Pullman cars which formed the new train. After lunch served on the train, the party was met with a reception at Ramsgate organised by the mayor who said that "it was evident that under the mantle of the new British Railways the old Southern Railway had lost none of its capacity for commercial betterment." The dignitaries were then taken on a short tour by motor coach around the area before returning to London on the up service.

From 1951 three coaches were detached at Faversham and ran separately through to Canterbury East with the name of the train being altered to the more geographically accurate "Kentish Belle". However, due to lack of demand this Canterbury leg was withdrawn after just a year but the new title for the train was retained until the end of the summer service in 1958 when the named service was discontinued due to the impending Kent Coast electrification. Subsequently the 11:35am from Victoria merely carried the timetable note 'Includes limited Pullman car facilities'. The "Devon Belle" had already operated for the final time four years earlier in 1954 leaving just the Bournemouth and Brighton services to carry on the full Pullman tradition on the Southern region. The Bournemouth service went with the end of steam on the SR in July 1967 whilst the "Brighton Belle" soldiered on until retired in April 1972.

Top: Still displaying the smokebox Southern roundel, Battle of Britain No. 21C168 *Kenley* enters Margate passing 'B' signal cabin with the up service in June 1948. It would be renumbered to 34068 in September.
IMAGE SOURCE: JCFF5-3

Bottom: The corridor connection on the rear carriage was adorned with a tailboard depicting the Pullman logo and the name of the new service, and carriage roofboards also advertised the train.
IMAGE SOURCE: JCFF6-2

Opposite page: Displaying the headboard, No. 21C157 *Biggin Hill* passes Margate up advanced starter and Westgate-on-Sea distant at 5:10pm on 15 June 1948 with the up service.
IMAGE SOURCE: N7/1

Atlantic abomination

The graceful atlantic 4-4-2s of the LB&SCR were much admired for their aesthetically pleasing lines so it was with a sense of shock that railwaymen and enthusiasts saw one of their number subjected to such disfiguring treatment as the replacement of its Stephenson slide valve gear with sleeve valves. This indignity was inflicted upon No. 32039, originally named *La France* in 1913, prior to working a train from Portsmouth carrying the French President Raymond Poincare on a visit to the UK, and subsequently renamed *Hartland Point* in 1926. No. 32039 had been one of the original five atlantics designated Class H1 and designed by Douglas Earle Marsh with construction taking place in 1905/6. A further five, this time with superheaters, larger cylinders and a reduced boiler pressure, were constructed in 1911/12 and classed as H2. A sixth locomotive which Marsh had intended to be constructed as a four cylinder variant was actually built to the normal two cylinder format of the other five. They proved popular and versatile machines, giving good service for many years, but following the end of World War 2 they were increasingly relegated to secondary duties so it was perhaps in view of their age and the fact that taking one out of regular traffic for experimentation would be no great loss to the operating department that one of their number was chosen as a testbed for one of the more controversial aspects of Bulleid's revolutionary "Leader" concept. Simply put, the CME's wish to incorporate sleeve valve technology was done in an effort to increase the efficiency of steam usage by reducing losses caused by condensation. Deciding that no marked increase in thermal efficiency could be expected from developments with orthodox piston valves, he had been impressed by the Sabre engines, that had incorporated sleeve valves, of the Hawker Typhoon aircraft which his son had flown for the RAF. However, as it turned out, aircraft engines and locomotive engines were very different kettles of fish.

No. 2039, as it was then numbered entered Brighton Works in July 1947 for multiple modifications at Bulleid's behest, emerging on 5 November "resplendent" with sleeve valves, new cylinders, outside steam pipes, mechanical lubricators and a fabricated wide chimney to accept a five jet Lemaitre blastpipe, all of which radically altered its appearance, also much of the running plate around the front end had to be removed. In addition the front bogie had to be replaced as it would have fouled the new cylinders. The replacement came in the form of a bogie from a D3 tank locomotive and the Westinghouse brake pump position was moved. As it was Bulleid's intention to fit six sets of sleeve valve gear to his Leader, he was keen to gauge the effectiveness of such a radical concept applied to steam locomotives before committing them to the revolutionary 0-6-0+0-6-0T. It made a number of test trips before the year end by which time it was back in Brighton Works for modification. However it emerged on 1 January , the first day of the new nationalised railway system, and as Jeremy English describes in his book on the Brighton Atlantics, *'Little did the new public body realise that this was a harbinger (albeit an innocent one) of its first great public relations disaster!'* i.e. the Leader fiasco.

The 1948 tests began with a series of trips hauling an empty three coach carriage set between Brighton and Eastbourne, no doubt wishing to keep things locally handy for Brighton Works should things go awry. Tests between Brighton and Groombridge followed but, in the absence of any formal records having survived it is not possible

Opposite top: Parked up and still sporting Southern on the tender and carrying cabside No. 2039 the 'guinea pig' atlantic, officially still named Hartland Point, presents a woeful sight at Brighton shed with enlarged chimney and sleeve valves doing nothing for its appearance. IMAGE SOURCE: MP50333

Opposite bottom: No. 2039 in steam, after having completed one of its test runs, is captured on the turntable located at the side of Brighton shed. IMAGE SOURCE: RCR1539

to categorically state how things went but it appears that 70mph was easily achieved and maintained. Light engine tests up the main Brighton – London line, in the company of a K Class mogul as insurance in case of breakdown on this busy main line, followed later in January. The following month saw sufficient confidence gained to allow the "guinea pig" H1 to handle trains of carriage underframes from Lancing Carriage Works to Eastleigh. These runs showed up significantly increased water and coal consumption, often necessitating two water stops in just 65 miles, the gallons used/mile figure being some 3½ times what would be considered normal. Back in Brighton Works by the end of the month further modifications were made but by March she was out on the road again visiting Lewes, Cowden and Hastings amongst other locations. In June a three coach load was taken from Brighton to Tunbridge Wells West. The load was increased to four or five coaches until July. Details of runs later in the year are sketchy but it is believed that No. 2039 spent much of the time inside the Works where most of the workforce's attention was focussed on continuing the output of light pacifics and of course on No. 36001.

December 1948 saw further light engine runs to Hastings whilst on the 19th of the month an Officers' special from Ashford to Brighton was, perhaps rashly, entrusted to No. 2039. On leaving St. Leonards there was a fracture of the right hand valve rod following which the motion had to be completely taken down in the nearby shed and the locomotive ignominiously towed back to Brighton. That was it for 1948 and it was not until 14 March 1949 that it was noted again, this time on the Brighton – Redhill leg of the Hastings – Birkenhead service. This was apparently the only occasion on which 2039 worked a fare paying passenger service successfully. By the spring of 1949 the first Leader was ready so the services of 2039 were no longer required. It re-entered the Works ostensibly with the idea of removing the sleeve valves and accoutrements and reverting to its original form, however, as by this date it was virtually life expired no further work was ever done on it other than a repaint into plain black livery and renumbering as 32039. Although theoretically released back to traffic it is doubtful if it was ever used again, spending most of its time parked up at Brighton together with partly completed Leaders Nos. 36002-5 quietly rusting away until February 1951 when it was briefly reallocated to Bricklayers Arms, on paper at least, before being taken to Eastleigh for scrapping in March. The performance of sleeve valve technology on the Leader is of course very much a story for another day.

(With grateful thanks to Kevin Robertson for permission to quote details of the test runs of No. 2039 in 1948 as detailed in his book 'The Leader Project – Fiasco or Triumph')

Opposite: A close up of the sleeve valve 'gubbins' and associated pipework foisted on poor old No. 2039. The piston still operated fore and aft but steam admission and exhaust was now via a separate sleeve valve surrounding the piston which also moved forwards and back at the same time as rotating slightly up and down - the amount of up and down movement may be gauged by the slots in the sleeve guides. Sleeve valve engines gave, in theory at least, a more efficient use of the piston with the inlet gases, in this case steam, less chance of cooling and consequently greater efficiency (expansion) was achieved. Fine in theory but the big disadvantage was lubrication; hence Bulleid's attempt at insurance with numerous oil delivery pipes provided. The latter were fed from two mechanical lubricators sited of all places under the smokebox door and so prone to ash ingress whenever the covers were removed. Greater efficiency was thus hoped for but at the expense of added complications. Would it work? Time would tell, but Bulleid had already committed his Leader design to the same type of valve even before 'Hartland Point' ran its first test. It was a gamble from the outset. IMAGE SOURCE: REV 4983-3

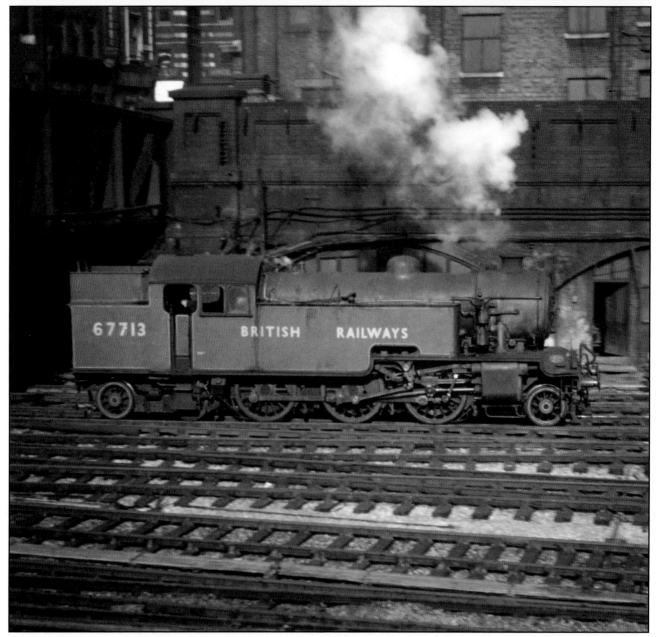

Above: An almost new L1 class No. 67713 is seen at Liverpool Street in June 1948 resplendent in green livery with yellow lettering showing its number and new owner. It had been completed at Darlington Works a couple of months previously as E9012 and had been renumbered in May, being initially allocated to Stratford shed. IMAGE SOURCE: REV001

Opposite top: 'Sandringham' or 'Footballer' Class No. 61665 *Leicester City*, renumbered in July 1948, and B1 No. 61058, renumbered in September 1948, are seen at a very smoky and grimy Liverpool Street. IMAGE SOURCE: REV081

Opposite bottom: The Tyneside Electrics were suburban railways that the NER and later the LNER electrified using a third rail system from 1904 onwards. Electric services from Newcastle were extended to South Shields in 1938. The LNER 1937 stock seen above remained in service with BR until 1955 when new stock on the South Tyneside line based on SR 2-EPB stock was introduced. This rare colour view shows an electric set at Newcastle Central in September 1948. IMAGE SOURCE: REV188

Photographed at Eastleigh shed SR King Arthur class No. 740 *Merlin* is seen with oil tank mounted in the tender. This locomotive was converted to oil on 14 December 1946 and re-converted back to coal on 20 October 1948. Adjacent is another locomotive with oil tank also visible in the tender, the installation of which did nothing for the aesthetics of the original tender design. The Southern had joined in the move to oil with enthusiasm, starting with an experiment on a 'Terrier' tank and quickly moving on to several Drummond 4-4-0 designs, two 'King Arthur' engines and two 'West Country' types. They were based around Eastleigh and Fratton although the plan had been to provide Exmouth Junction with refuelling facilities. No depot infrastructure was ever fully complete although Fratton came the closest when the scheme was abandoned. The converted engines were to be seen working services as far afield as Bournemouth, Waterloo, Salisbury, Andover, Portsmouth and Southampton, usually with reasonable success. Some failures did occur, often in consequence of a crew being unfamiliar with the method of operating - such as when one driver and fireman deliberately let the flame out and then found neither carried any matches. There was also discussion about converting Bath Green Park to an oil only depot, the thought of crews having to contend with oil fumes through the narrow bore Somerset & Dorset line tunnels - the stuff of nightmares!
IMAGE SOURCE: R H G SIMPSON

*Details of initial planned conversions (subject to change)

GWR - 172 locomotives comprising 2-8-0 class 28xx; 4-6-0 Hall class; 4-6-0 Castle class. These are in addition to the 44 already converted under the company's own programme.
LMS – 485 locomotives comprising Class 5 4-6-0MT; Class 4 0-6-0; Class 7 0-8-0; Class 7 2-8-0; Class 8 2-8-0; 2-6-6-2 Garratt.
LNER – 450 locomotives comprising Ministry of Supply Class O1, O2 and O4 2-8-0s; J39 0-6-0; K3 2-6-0; Q6 0-8-0.
SR – 110 locomotives comprising West Country; N15; H15; N; U; D15; L11; T9 classes.

Oil conversion scheme scrapped

A Central Office of Information film entitled 'Britain can make it' issued in 1946 began with these words delivered in the rather clipped tones of the period of course – *'Britain's greatest shortage today is coal and the Ministry of Fuel and Parr (!) looked round for ways of saving it and found one way on the railways. As a temporary measure all railways are asked to follow the example of the Great Western and convert 1,200* engines over to oil burning'*. The conversion process entailed the boiler being lifted to enable oil jets to be fitted and the coal bunker in the tender being replaced with an oil tank. Many dirty time consuming jobs associated with coal were thus dispensed with and no longer would a fireman be required to shovel a ton of coal on average every 50 miles. He could, in the words of the film, *"sit twiddling the knobs to meet his driver's needs"*. Refuelling time was reduced by two thirds and a little steam from an adjacent locomotive blown through the burner atomised the oil and a small wad of burning waste was used to light the fire, the whole process, as the commentator states, being *"As simple as lighting a guess jit (!)"*. When the conversion programme was completed it was anticipated that 1m tons of coal p.a. would be saved thus improving supplies to industry and to the homes of Britain. The fuel situation had been exacerbated by the rise in the price and the deterioration in the quality of coal produced during the war and would subsequently be affected by the severe winter of 1947/8. In 1945 the Anglo-Iranian Oil Co. became involved with the GWR's own oil conversion programme, assisting in the conversion of heavy freight 2-8-0s and later some of the Castle class. The Ministry of Supply provided all the equipment for the conversion programme, having placed an order with the North British Locomotive Co. Ltd. for 1,192 sets of materials including firepans, brickwork, fire-doors, manifolds, steam and oil piping, valves etc. In addition 715 oil tanks complete with heaters were also ordered from North British whilst others were supplied by Royal Ordnance factories and dockyards. The LMS calculated that the cost of converting their 485 locomotives would be of the order of £900k.

However, one year later in September 1947 when just 93 locomotives had been converted the Ministry of Transport was informed that the 840,000 tons of oil required yearly for the full programme might not be available and, indeed there were doubts about Britain's supplies of foreign currency and therefore its ability to pay for it. At the beginning of 1948 the BTC reported that the oil required for the locomotives so far converted would add £279k p.a. to running costs and that the full programme would cost a massive £3.5m p.a. In January a "postponement" order was given to the effect that no further conversions should be undertaken. The scheme was formally abandoned in May 1948 and the locomotives so far converted were re-converted back to burn coal, the reconversion costs being approximately £200/locomotive. The oil storage depots so far constructed were placed on a "care and maintenance" basis costing some £10k p.a. and it was said that the position would be reviewed in October. But that was in fact the end of a scheme which, in the report of the Comptroller & Auditor General for y/e 31 March 1948, was reported to have cost the Ministry of Transport and ultimately the taxpayer some £3m.

1948 was not quite the end of the story however as there were a couple more cases of coal to oil conversion in subsequent years, namely the former LNER Garratt in 1952 and a solitary pannier tank, No. 3711, which was oil fired during 1958-9. Although the Government and BR may have got their fingers badly burned with the conversion programme of the 1940s, this did not deter them from experimenting with early diesel and gas turbine locomotives, leading to the later wholesale dieselisation programme that effectively spelled the end for the steam locomotive.

Curtains for the Corris

After weeks of speculation and a couple of press reports which appeared in the Montgomery County Times on 31 July and in the Liverpool Daily Post of 24 August, it seems likely that the former narrow gauge Corris Railway, built to the unusual 2ft. 3in. gauge, has closed without notice. After what proved to be the final goods train, running on 20 August, services were suspended and it now seems unlikely that they will be resumed following flood damage to a part of the line. Although some reports indicate that this damage was slight, it has been claimed by the Western region of BR, who were in any event reluctant inheritors of the system upon nationalisation earlier this year, that the cost of repairs necessary to strengthen a bridge over the river is likely to prove prohibitive bearing in mind that the line has been losing money for many years. Although the river did begin to undermine the Corris Railway embankment on the south side of the Dovey Bridge, the track was never breached however this was enough of a reason apparently for BR to close the line. Fortunately the likelihood of flooding of the River Dovey (Afon Dyfi) had been anticipated and two of the line's locomotives, 0-4-2STs, Nos. 3 and 4, had been moved to Machynlleth and stored under tarpaulins to avoid being cut off. Track on the Aberllefenni to Corris section was lifted in November and the 10 tons of the rail recovered was later purchased by Henry Haydn Jones for use on his Talyllyn Railway. By the end of 1950 track lifting had reached the Machynlleth terminus.

Opening in 1859 as a horse tramway, the line served a number of slate quarries although the closure of Braichgoch Quarry in 1906 saw the railway return its first operating loss and, although the line continued on through subsequent decades, serving the quarries around Corris and Aberllefenni, it never again showed a profit. As well as an outward traffic in slate, the line hauled timber extracted from the Dyfi forest from the 1910s through to the 1930s and carried coal and general goods inwards to the quarries whilst serving the scattered communities along the line. The concern was sold to the GWR in 1929 who promptly began running a bus service in competition with the railway, leading to the withdrawal of the passenger service in 1931. Seventeen years later we have seen the end of yet another piece of unique narrow gauge railway history. *(Ed: Although today of course there is a flourishing preservation society based at Corris and operating between there and Maespoeth, over 1 mile of track with plans to extend further southwards. Both ex-Corris Railway locomotives, Nos. 3 and 4, can be found on the Talyllyn Railway.)*

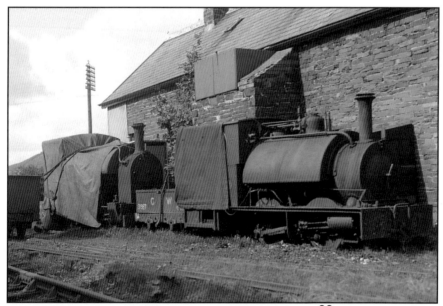

Parked out of use under tarpaulins at Machynlleth in 1948 are Corris Railway locomotives Nos. 3 and 4.
IMAGE SOURCE: NS208866A

Passengers no more on the East Kent railway

One of the few minor lines which was nationalised was the East Kent Railway which, along with the Kent & East Sussex Railway, passed to the Southern region, the others being the Mersey Railway passing to the Midland region and the Shropshire & Montgomeryshire Railway which passed to the Western region. The recently issued Southern region winter timetable, operative from 27 September 1948, omitted all mention of a passenger service over the East Kent line as it had been intended to withdraw the service at the end of September. However, it was decided to continue to offer passengers the opportunity to ride its trains until the end of October with the final service, carrying a grand total of five passengers, running on the evening of Saturday 30 October. This railway linked the Kent coalfield with the main line of the Southern region at Shepherdswell near Dover. Passenger traffic on the line was always of secondary importance and towards the end was negligible given the very basic service of just two trains each way daily from Shepherdswell to the terminus at Wingham which had operated since 1931. It had originally been intended to extend the line from Wingham to Canterbury but this was never carried out. Departures were at 7:30am, 5pm (SX), 6:03pm (SO) from Shepherdswell, returning from Wingham (Canterbury Road) at 8:40am, 6:20pm (SX), 6:50pm (SO) with a notional journey time of 42 minutes for the 11 miles 27 chains covered. Freight traffic will continue to be handled by BR from Tilmanstone colliery to Shepherdswell. *(Ed: Such traffic lasted until the miners' strike of 1984. The colliery closed in 1986 and the line was officially closed at the end of 1987.)*

With the legend EKR still just about visible on the tender, EKR No. 6 has a typical train of the period comprising just one coach and a van seen here at the EKR terminus at Shepherdswell. This 0-6-0 was built in 1891 by Sharp, Stewart and was ex-SE&C Class O No. 372. Purchased from the Southern Railway in 1923, it was re-numbered 6 by the EKR. It was rebuilt to the O1 class specification in 1932 and after inheritance by BR in 1948 was allocated No. 31372 although this was never applied. It was withdrawn in February 1949 and scrapped at Ashford the same month.
IMAGE SOURCE: MP80607

EKR locomotive No. 2 was an 0-6-0ST built in 1908 by Hudswell Clark for the WC&PR. Before transfer to the EKR in 1913 it had worked on the S&MR. After a loan to the PD&SWR in 1917 it was sold for scrap in 1943 but later worked at Purfleet Deep Water Wharf and Hastings Gas Works before being scrapped in 1957. IMAGE SOURCE: NS208823

EKR locomotive No. 7 was an 0-6-0ST built in 1882 by Beyer, Peacock. Having served with both the L&SWR and the War Office it was purchased by the EKR in 1926, lasting in traffic until 1944. It was then sold to the Southern Railway but soon scrapped at Ashford Works in March of that year. IMAGE SOURCE: NS208825

End of the line for passengers on the Easingwold railway

One of the earliest line closures to passengers, following the recent railway nationalisation, involved the short 2½ mile branch line, often referred to as England's shortest branch line, from Alne on the East Coast Main Line (ECML) to the Vale of York market town of Easingwold. After several failed attempts to have the ECML routed near to or through the town, a privately owned branch line was opened in 1891 from Easingwold to the main line at Alne. First proposed back in 1836, it was not until some half a century later in 1887 that a consortium of local businessmen formed a railway company and obtained parliamentary approval for construction. The first contractor, appropriately named De'ath and Company, failed with a second contractor finally opening the line on 27 July 1891 and thereafter the line remained privately owned making small profits until road competition bit into its returns in the late 1940s. Although always closely associated with the former NER and its successor LNER, it continued to retain its independence even after the recent nationalisation. Known by the locals as 'T'awd coffeepot', the passenger service had, by 1947, declined to just two return trips daily so perhaps this announcement of withdrawal comes as no surprise. Following the voluntary liquidation of the company, with debts of £17,000, BR stated that goods and parcels traffic will continue. *(Ed: They did until the end of 1957 when complete closure occurred.)*

Left: This old grounded coach body was on the approach to Easingwold station which is seen in the right distance in this view dating from 1943. IMAGE SOURCE: RCR1185

Right: Nine years later the end came for freight services over the Easingwold line, as this 27 December 1957 view of the closure notice fixed to the gable of the station building shows. IMAGE SOURCE: MM438

EASINGWOLD STATION

On and from 28ᵗʰ December 1957
Easingwold Station will cease
to be open for traffic in full
truck loads and alternative
facilities will be provided at
ALNE station
A British Railways Office
will be open from 9.30am to R.om
each weekday for the acceptance of
parcels hiring of sacks and enquires

For further information see Amoldt

A re-opening of sorts

Saughtree station, situated on the branch from Hexham to Riccarton Junction which was closed on 1 December 1944 as a wartime economy measure, was not re-opened until 23 August 1948, some three years after the conclusion of hostilities. Although no doubt glad to see the return of their trains, the service provided for the local population can hardly be said to have been generous however, as they saw just one northbound train, the 11:20 am from Newcastle to Hawick, which called only on Mondays and Thursdays, to pick up only, at 1:45pm, three minutes later on Saturdays, and one southbound working, the 4:30pm Hawick to Newcastle, which set down only on similar weekdays at 5:08pm, two minutes later on Saturdays. At least this allowed shoppers a few hours in the market town of Hawick on three days a week. *(Ed: Saughtree station is currently preserved as a B&B establishment with 1/3 mile of track, a Ruston diesel and a couple of wagons on site.)*

Lonely Saughtree station was a mile or so from the small village of the same name and was generally untroubled by stopping trains on the former Border Counties Railway. Having re-opened in 1948, it closed to passengers just over 8 years later on 15 October 1956. IMAGE SOURCE: NS205984

Scottish border floods

The 'Glorious Twelth' traditionally signifies the start of the grouse season in August each year but another event assumed an even greater importance in Scotland and the 12 August 1948 turned out to be anything but 'glorious'. Described at the time as the greatest natural disaster to hit the Borders region of Scotland after several days of intermittent heavy rain, catastrophic downpours on the 11 and 12 August caused many parts of Berwickshire to receive one third of their annual rainfall in the space of just six days. Following torrential rain on what became known as 'Black Friday August 13', the rivers Tweed, Blackadder, Whiteadder, Till and Eye Water all overflowed causing huge amounts of damage, and low lying farmland near the small village of Ayton was turned into a giant inland lake estimated to be more than a mile long, 30ft deep and containing 4 million tons of water. This lake was only held back by a 60ft high embankment on the main Berwick to Edinburgh railway line, leading to fears that the embankment could collapse,

causing water to rush down a gorge into the nearby coastal town of Eyemouth. A trench fitted with sluice gates was dug through the embankment and special pumps were installed to release the impounded water in a controlled fashion, lowering the water level by 2ft. at a time until half the volume of water had been dealt with. The Metropolitan Water Board was then summoned from London to render assistance with their specialist equipment which pumped the remaining water safely away thus averting the collapse of the nearby railway embankment. This operation took five weeks to accomplish and was a remarkable effort of co-operation amongst various agencies.

The ECML was blocked at several points in Northumberland at Chathill, Little Mill, Belford and between Goswick and Scremerston. Further north there were blockages between Berwick and Dunbar whilst at Burnmouth there were two major slips with considerable resultant damage to the

Ayton lake, the body of water created after days of rain, was held back by the adjoining railway embankment of the ECML.
IMAGE SOURCE IN THIS SECTION: LORNE ANTON / AYTON LOCAL HISTORY SOCIETY

tracks. Between Reston and Grantshouse seven bridges were washed away and the foundations of a further four between Cockburnspath and Dunbar were undermined. Additionally in this area there were two landslides, one washout and four cases of serious subsidence underneath the trackbed. Army assistance in the shape of the Royal Engineers was called in to help and to erect wartime Bailey Bridges in order to allow many routes to re-open. Dinghies loaned by the RAF were used by railway engineers making surveys of the damage. As can be imagined this was a massive operation, with the main line remaining closed for 11 weeks, leading to a railway repair bill estimated at the time to be £300,000 for the work currently being undertaken with a further £400,000 for the future replacement of temporary bridges by permanent structures. This is the equivalent of £28m today and when other repairs to road bridges and damage to property, etc. are taken into account it is estimated that the total repair bill for all damage caused by the floods would have topped £40m at today's prices. Main and branch lines of both the North Eastern and Scottish regions of BR were affected with the ECML being blocked at eleven places over a thirty mile stretch between Newcastle and Edinburgh. In addition, long lengths of embankment adjoining the vanished bridges were also eroded away leaving gaps of up to 150 feet across the river. Long lengths of both track and ballast were washed away between Grantshouse and Cockburnspath with great quantities of debris deposited on the line. In a forerunner of the infamous Dawlish storm some 71 years later, where track was left suspended in mid-air, track on the ECML similarly suffered with track hanging unsupported over several gaps. Track suspension also occurred on the Waverley route where several culverts had become unsafe and rails were left hanging over chasms 15ft. deep whilst at Galashiels floodwater carried tons of debris through the station.

Many trains were marooned part way through their journeys and passengers had to complete their trips by road. During the period that the main line was closed services to Edinburgh were diverted some via Newcastle, Carlisle and Carstairs, and later some via Kelso, St. Boswells and the Waverley route. The 'Flying Scotsman' was diverted from Newcastle to Carlisle on 13 August and then proceeded via the Waverley route but only reached Hawick where it was found that the route northwards at Galashiels was also blocked. It perforce had to retrace its steps to Carlisle and the exhausted passengers finally reached Edinburgh via Carstairs some ten hours later than scheduled at 3:15 in the morning. Diversions via Carlisle continued until 16 August, resulting in much congestion with trains queuing outside the station, when southbound trains were diverted via St. Boswells and Kelso to reach Tweedmouth on the ECML, this route being adopted for all Anglo-Scottish services on 23 August when temporary timetables came into force. On 24 and 25 August for example, A4 No. 60028 *Walter K Whigham* undertook up and down runs on both days with the non-stop 'Flying Scotsman' service and it must have been quite a sight to see these "expresses" trundling along the single line section between St. Boswells and Kelso.

Tweedmouth was selected as the railhead for the collection of engineering materials brought up from the Central Reclamation Depot at Darlington where parts sourced from all regions were sorted before transfer to the affected area. In many cases the only access to affected sites was by road and materials were thus brought in and stored in dumps located at the affected locations. The number of the workforce employed soon reached 600 and the ECML was re-opened as far north as Berwick upon Tweed on 14 August but with single line working in force between Goswick and Tweedmouth for a few days. The Waverley route saw restoration on 16 August with single line working on some sections. With temporary bridges in place, restoration of working north of Berwick did not occur until 25 October for freight and 1 November for passenger traffic. Prior to re-opening weight tests were carried out on the temporary bridges employing A4 pacific No. 60012 *Commonwealth of Australia* and D49 No. 62706 *Forfarshire* coupled together giving a combined weight of some 280 tons. Both were allocated to Edinburgh's Haymarket depot at the time. The first freight train allowed through was hauled by K3 No. 61992 from Edinburgh's St. Margaret's depot

Opposite top: This view of the entrance to the reinforced cutting through the embankment was taken from the lake side on 29 August 1948.
Opposite bottom: Reinforcing the cutting through the embankment.

and the first 'Flying Scotsman' to regain its former route on 1 November was headed by A3 pacific No. 60060 *The Tetrarch*. Temporary speed restrictions of between 15-30mph were in force at several locations until permanent bridges, which were not expected until the summer of 1949, could be constructed. Repair of the branch line damage was naturally afforded a lower priority and consequently many saw long delays in their re-opening. Both the Gifford and Lauder branches, goods only by this time, suffered damage to bridges with the section from Gifford to Humbie subsequently closing completely. The Lauder branch re-opened in November 1950. The centre pier on a viaduct located on the line from Burnmouth to Eyemouth was undermined and dislodged although fortunately the girders resting upon it were not damaged enabling the line to be re-opened in June 1949. The cross country route from St. Boswells to Reston was also damaged in many places and the passenger service was promptly cut back to serve just the Reston – Duns section. A couple of fascinating films of the time, one a short Pathe Newsreel and the other, commissioned by BR and introduced by the Chairman Sir Eustace Missenden which runs for 22 minutes, can be viewed on the internet. In the latter film entitled "Floods in the North" Missenden states that the film serves a threefold purpose and I can do no better than quote his words. *"Firstly it places on record some of the major effects of one of the greatest disasters of nature upon a vital part of the railway system. Secondly it shows how the immediate emergency thus created was met by administrative improvisation on the one side and on the other by resolute courage and devotion to duty on the part of the staff on the ground. Thirdly it shows how the co-ordinated resources of the unified British Railways were brought into play with the utmost speed to meet the emergency."*

(Ed: Had the railways not been newly nationalised one wonders how the LNER might have managed the disaster using just its own resources.) Sir Eustace, together with the aptly named Mr. J. C. L. Train, member of the Railway Executive for Civil Engineering, came to inspect the progress before the line was re-opened to passenger traffic, being transported to various sites in coaches hauled by B1 Class No. 1255. As a token of BR's esteem a small ceremony hosted by the Chief regional Officer of the Scottish region, Mr. T. F. Cameron, was subsequently held to honour twenty of the men intimately concerned with operations in the flood area at which awards of watches and fountain pens were distributed.

Opposite top: This improvised but effective exit chute leading from the reinforced cut made through the railway embankment at Ayton. Water started being released from the lake in a controlled manner at 12:15 on the afternoon of Sunday 29 August and can be seen cascading down the chute.

Opposite bottom: Metropolitan Water Board pumps discharging water from Ayton lake.

Top: When bridge No. 133 was washed away between Grantshouse and Reston, the track was left suspended as in this view taken shortly afterwards on 15 August. As Robbie Burns put it 'The best-laid schemes o' mice and men gang aft agley' and they certainly went 'agley' here on the ECML in August 1948.

Bottom: Flooding in the station area and debris on the track in the distance attracts the attention of sightseers on the bridge at Grantshouse station on 15 August.

Top: The dramatic results of a collapsed culvert, No. 146, located some 1½ miles west of the village of Ayton.

Bottom: Progress of work to reconstruct bridge No. 133, known as Freekirk bridge, was photographed on 13 October.

TESTING BRIDGE 126 (PHOTOGRAPHED 21-10-48).

Opposite top: On 21 October, Class D49 4-4-0 No. 62706 *Forfarshire* tests the embankment next to bridge No. 90 with its new north west wing wall in place, constructed by the firm of Ivan Tait, contractor.

Opposite bottom: Two locomotives in the shape of A4 No. 60012 and D49 No. 62706 were used to test bridge No. 126 situated between Grantshouse and Reston. By this time the former torrent had subsided to something like its normal level.

This page top: When natty headgear was de rigueur Sir Eustace Missenden, sporting the leather gloves, and his party meet local railway officials at Ayton station during the inspection tour of 26 October 1948.

Site of embankment breach.

Site of Ayton lake.

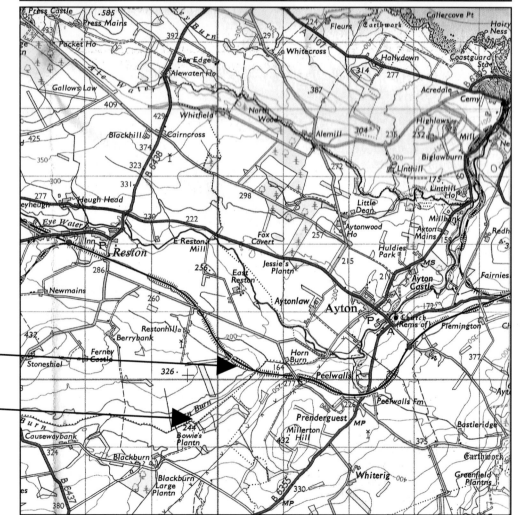

Canadian pathetic

Bulleid had been keen to try out a mechanical stoker on one of his Merchant Navy pacifics but with the interruption of World War 2 it was not until October 1947 that the Southern Railway took delivery of a reconditioned Berkeley mechanical stoker, the American company conveniently having representation in the UK. On 18 March 1948 Eastleigh Works fitted this contraption to No. 21C5, appropriately enough named *Canadian Pacific* given that these devices were common in North America, and which was to be renumbered 35005 the following month. A coal pusher located in the tender forced the coal, which was desirably of a uniform size, forwards to a screw, effectively a coal crusher, which passed the fuel to a distributor plate fitted in the firehole door from where it was transferred to various parts of the firebox by steam jets which ensured that coal was delivered over the whole area of the grate. The screw was driven by a steam engine located in the tender with the quantity of coal delivered being controlled by the speed of this stoker engine. The firehole door was not obstructed by this apparatus so that hand firing could still be undertaken if required and a number of "peep-holes" located in the firehole door allowed the fire to be observed without opening the doors. Strangely this contraption was reckoned to be almost silent in operation! A number of trials were run from Eastleigh shed - handy for the Works of course should anything go wrong. After a brief spell in the Works for further attention, No. 35005 was transferred to Nine Elms where it ran close on 60,000 miles before coming back to Eastleigh for a heavy intermediate overhaul.

Contrary to some published reports the locomotive did not travel to the new Locomotive Testing Station at Rugby, see article in this volume detailing the locomotives tested here which reveals that the only Merchant Navy to visit was No. 35022 in 1952. No. 35005 was subject to road testing using the former LMS Mobile Test Plant between Wimbledon and Salisbury. These tests were completed by 4 April 1950 when the mechanical stoker was removed to allow comparative tests with hand firing. The stoker was replaced on 31 May 1950 and a report of the road

The cab of 35005 showing the installation of the mechanical stoker.

tests was issued on 25 August 1950, details of which were published by O.S. Nock in the magazine 'The Engineer' in October 1950. The report concluded that "For normal English conditions of firing with typical grades of coal the mechanical stoker is less efficient in working than hand firing though the difference is less marked when using poor quality coal." The stoker was finally removed in March/April 1951 although further trials, this time with Standard Class 9Fs, did result in similar mechanical stokers being fitted to Nos. 92165-7 with No. 92166 being tested at Rugby at the end of 1958. Needless to say the various crews of No. 35005 were not enamoured of such a new fangled piece of kit, especially as they only came into contact with it intermittently when rostered to this particular locomotive. That they christened it 'Canadian Pathetic' was not perhaps entirely unexpected.

Rugby locomotive testing station (LTS)

Ernest Moore, one of the elite set of men who acted as a Royal Train driver on occasions, carefully reversed his gleaming A4 No. 60007 into the shed. This task was made somewhat easier in the absence of the pacific's tender which had been removed earlier in the day. The locomotive came to a halt and rollers, which were fitted with a profile similar to rails and could be electrically operated to replicate different loads and conditions, were raised to lift the wheels off the track, a speedometer driving disc was fitted and all was ready for the demonstration for this was 16 October 1948, the day of the opening ceremony of the Rugby Locomotive Testing Station. Once all the preliminaries had been completed the Minister of Transport, Alfred Barnes, in the company of various officials of the Ministry of Transport and of the newly formed Rail Executive together with the Mayor of Rugby and other local dignitaries, entered the building. After inspecting the locomotive and the test bed they ascended to the control platform and after a short speech the Minister declared the plant open by pulling on a cord attached to the A4's chime whistle. It was fitting perhaps that the locomotive chosen to christen this new facility was No. 60007, named of course after Sir Nigel Gresley who, though he did not live to see the project realised having died in 1941, was the leading proponent of such a testing station. Also present in the yard for a short time, and taking no part in the opening, was No. 46256 *Sir William A. Stanier F.R.S.* as if to reinforce the message that this was very much a joint LNER/LMS venture.

This October day was the end result of a long campaign begun by the CME of the former LNER back in 1927 during his presidential address to the Institution of Locomotive Engineers. Although a committee was formed to investigate the possibility of such a facility and a site had been earmarked on the outskirts of Leeds, unfortunately by the time the committee reported the dire economic situation of the early 1930s militated against the government coming up with any finance for such a venture. Neither the GWR, who had enjoyed their own testing plant at Swindon since 1905, nor the Southern, whose main focus was electrification, could be cajoled into joining forces to fund a national testing station. In December 1934 recourse was had to a plant located at Vitry in the suburbs of Paris which had opened the previous year, when the LNER's 2-8-2 *Cock o' the North* was shipped over, along with a certain observer named Oliver Bulleid, for testing. By 1937 the economic situation had improved somewhat and the LNER and LMS decided to join forces and build a testing station at Rugby. A site was chosen between the main line to Euston, adjacent to the motive power depot and repair shops, and close to the viaduct of the former Great Central route from which a spur was planned thus facilitating access for even the heaviest locomotives of both companies. The contract for supplying the equipment was let to the engineering firm of Heenan & Froude of Worcester which had been founded back in 1881 in Newton Heath, Manchester. Unfortunately the advent of war in 1939 halted the construction programme, which by that time was quite well advanced and the buildings were mothballed until they could be completed. Resuming after the ending of hostilities, the plant finally opened in 1948. A

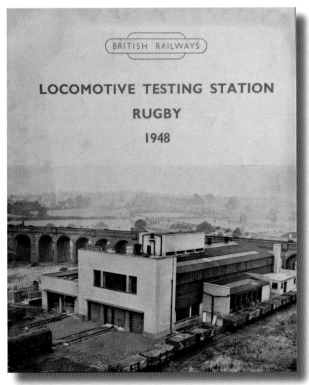

Front page of brochure produced by BR for the new LTS at Rugby.

A4 No 60007 *Sir Nigel Gresley* on the rollers at Rugby for press oblique demonstration purposes. The testing station could acommodate up to A10-Coupled engine; such as a 9F. Note the shoot taking the exhaust from the chimney was moveable, however no such prevision was available for the safety rails. The presence of the A4 was purely for publicity and little in the way of technical testing was achieved.

plaque was mounted on a wall just inside the entrance attesting to the fact that the test plant equipment was supplied by Heenan & Froude. The site of some 7¾ acres contained two buildings, the larger of which was the Test House itself with an adjacent preparation shed coal bunker annexe, Foreman's office and mess room which were located over the boiler room of the heating installation. The second building, housing the chemical laboratory and offices, was near to, but separate from, the main building to reduce noise and vibration. A publicity brochure with a foreword by Sir Eustace Missenden, Chairman of the Railway Executive, was produced by BR to commemorate the opening of the plant. In his introductory remarks he paid tribute to the foresight of both Gresley and Stanier and he concluded by stating that, *"We are confident that it will prove an invaluable asset in the further evolution of the steam locomotive, in the most economical use of our coal resources for railway purposes, and in maintaining our country's position in the forefront of locomotive design and development."*

The deafening noise, steam and smoke of the testing station, even with its adjustable exhaust ventilators, made it an unpleasant place to linger for long. There were seven pairs of rollers supporting the locomotive, up to five of which would be driven by the locomotive's coupled wheels. Each of these five pairs of rollers was coupled to a "Froude" hydraulic brake or dynamometer capable of absorbing 1,200 hp and designed to cope with a maximum speed of 130mph. Considering the publicity brochure was produced for the layman as well as railway employees, it went into some considerable level of technical detail about the workings of the plant. Fortunately the instrument control room, where batteries of dials and indicators showed various outputs, was soundproofed and it also housed a permanent record of the locomotive's performance on graph paper for future study. Data on fuel consumption, hauling loads, behaviour on inclines and against wind resistance were typical of the test results recorded. The preparation shed with its inspection pits and wheel drop could undertake axle removal if required rendering it quite independent of outside technical assistance. The coal bunker annexe contained six bunkers, each of 12 ton capacity, and as the locomotives under test were lacking their tenders, the strictly monitored coal supply was via a firing platform containing a coal bunker and shovelling plate which could be raised or lowered to suit the fireman on the footplate. Water consumption from a calibrated tank was monitored by meters. There was a small workshop at the rear of the Test House where experimental fittings could be made and minor repairs undertaken. Finally there was a Drawing office where fittings were designed and where computation of test results and preparation of reports could be undertaken.

The demonstration runs of No. 60007 in October were to be followed in November by tests to calibrate the plant involving WD Austerity 2-10-0 No. 73799, built in 1945, which was renumbered to 90774 in 1948. Over the years testing of a number of different classes of locomotive took place including D49, B1, Black 5, Jubilee, Coronation and Royal Scot. Later types of BR Standard design were also tested including the Class 5, Britannia and 9F of single chimney, double chimney and Franco-Crosti boilered types. In 1952/3 the Southern region even got a look in when Merchant Navy No. 35022 underwent tests involving single and multiple jet blast pipes, although several sections of casing had to be removed from the air-smoothed Bulleid in order to permit access for instrumentation to be inserted to measure temperatures and pressures. In 1957/8 the gas turbine locomotive GT3, in an incomplete state, was taken to Rugby for testing both on the test rollers and on a short section of specially laid track afterwards returning to the Vulcan Foundry at Newton-le-Willows for completion. Parallel testing for comparative purposes out on the main line was also undertaken

on occasions as, for example, with the Merchant Navy and Coronation pacifics on the Skipton – Carlisle line.

From its inception in 1948 until the end of steam testing in 1959, the superintendent of the LTS was Denis Rock Carling who had formerly worked for Beyer Peacock before joining the Dynamometer Car section of the LNER in 1936. When steam locomotive testing finished in 1959 the alternative of mobile testing out on the track had become more sophisticated and was returning just as good results as testing on the stationary plant. Additionally, following improvements undertaken at Swindon in the 1950s, the test plant there could handle the increased power of the newer locomotives testing, for example, the 8P pacific *Duke of Gloucester* in October 1954. The Swindon facility continued in existence until closure of the Works complex in 1986. Rugby continued into the 1960s, testing diesel locomotives until 1965, although it did not formally close until 1970, the building latterly being increasingly derelict and unsafe with asbestos soundproofing hanging from its walls until demolition in 1984. Fortunately all its records are now held by the NRM in York.

Railway historians have long argued over whether building the LTS, with equipment costing over £200k at the time which equates to over £8m in today's money, was worth the effort. Perhaps ten years before in the late 1930s it would have made more sense but, with the interruption of World War II, the economics were undoubtedly more questionable in 1948 with diesel and electric power assuming greater importance. Although it had a relatively short useful life span, going from cutting edge to obsolescence in little more than a decade, there is no doubt that such tests did contribute to substantial improvements in steam traction in such areas as draughting, blast pipes, double chimneys, Giesl ejectors, superheating, mechanical stokers and in evaluating various types of valve gear such as Caprotti, Reidinger Poppet and Walschaerts. Today a small industrial estate occupies the site.

Locomotives tested at Rugby LTS 1948-1959

Class	No.	Date of initial test	Purpose of test
A4	60007	10/48	Demonstration only
WD 2-10-0	73799	11/48	Test plant calibration
Black Five	44752	1/49	Caprotti valve gear evaluation
WD 2-10-0	73788	4/49	Test plant calibration
D49	62764	5/49	Reidinger Poppet valve gear evaluation
Black Five	45218	1/50	Variation of valve lead tests
Black Five	44765	6/50	Single/ double chimneys
Black Five	44862	10/50	Dirty/ clean boiler alternatives
B1	61353	11/50	General performance/efficiency
Britannia	70005	4/51	General performance/efficiency
Standard Class 5	73008	8/51	General performance/efficiency
Merchant Navy	35022	3/52	Multiple/ single jet blastpipe
Britannia	70025	10/52	General performance/efficiency
St. Class 5	73030	7/53	General performance/efficiency
Hughes 2-6-0	42725	2/54	Comparison Reidinger/Walschaerts gear
Standard 9F	92013	5/54	Single chimney efficiency/performance
Standard 9F	92015	10/54	Reduced regulator opening tests
Hughes 2-6-0	42824	11/54	Comparison Reidinger/Walschaerts gear
Coronation	46225	1/55	General performance/ efficiency
Standard 9F	92023	6/55	Franco-Crosti boiler evaluation
Standard 9F	92050	10/55	General performance/ efficiency
Royal Scot	46165	12/55	General performance/ efficiency
Jubilee	45722	9/56	Improved draughting tests
Gas Turbine	GT3	7/57	General performance/efficiency
Standard Class 5	73031	2/58	Electrically augmented superheater
Standard 9F	92166	11/58	Berkley Mechanical stoker evaluation
St. 9F	92250	4/59	Double chimney/ Giesl ejector

Note: No. 92250 became the last steam locomotive to be tested at Rugby upon completion of the trials on 1 September 1959.

Royalty comes to Doncaster

In July 1948 an exhibition was held at Doncaster Works on the occasion of the visit of the Railway Queen. The first Railway Queen had been crowned as part of the centenary celebrations of the Stockton & Darlington railway back in 1925. The Queens of the early years were often daughters, aged between 14 -17, of railway workers and in 1947/8 the lucky girl was one 15 year old Janet Taylor of Leeds. The crowning took place in September of each year at Belle Vue Gardens in Manchester where the annual carnival of Railway Employees was held. Apart from the delights of viewing the Railway Queen, amongst other attractions on display at Doncaster that July were several locomotives including –

A4   60029 *Woodcock*

A1   60114 (only recently completed and later to be named W. P. Allen in October 1948)

A2   525   *A. H. Peppercorn*

Ex-GNR 4-4-2 No. 251 which was scheduled for preservation with its original livery restored. One of the famous Ivatt Atlantics, it had been withdrawn in July 1947 and can now be seen at the NRM

V2   60818 had just been renumbered from E818 after overhaul

Amid the bunting, No. 60029 *Woodcock* attracts the crowds queuing to gain access to the footplate of the A4 at Doncaster. IMAGE SOURCE: REV38B-6-4

Locomotive Running Dept. Southern Area coach No. 961800 had an interesting history. Starting life as a Director's saloon in 1883, it later became saloon No. 10 and in 1914 was converted to become an Instruction Coach, the first in the country, owned by the Great Eastern Railway and numbered EX3. The Great Central Railway introduced their own similar coach, now numbered 951650, soon afterwards and they toured their respective company's depots as "schools on wheels" for enginemen and providing instruction to aspiring drivers coming up for their examinations. With the grouping in 1923 both vehicles came under the LNER and in 1925 they were combined to operate as a two coach unit which they did until 1952 when they were overhauled at Doncaster and were joined by a third coach numbered 320043. The train contained a selection of many locomotive parts such as a Westinghouse brake, several of which were sectioned to show their inner workings. Models such as that of a superheater and diagrams were also used as teaching aids and part of the middle coach was fitted out as a classroom. It was withdrawn from service in 1964. IMAGE SOURCE: REV38B -6-5

Not a high-vis vest or safety helmet in sight and just imagine the risk assessments and safety cases that would have to be made these days to enable rides to be offered to the general public as BR were doing back in 1948 with the slogan 'Let British Railways give you a lift'. The board reads "Steam crane ride Adults 3d Children 2d." IMAGE SOURCE: REV38C-1-5

The cabside number and Doncaster brass worksplate adorn the cabside of recently completed A1 class No. 60114 not yet named *W.P.Allen*. IMAGE SOURCE: REV38C-2-3

Black 5 modifications

In addition to introducing a new class of 2-6-0, George Ivatt was keen to ensure that the workhorses of the former LMS, the Stanier Black Fives, were updated to keep abreast of the latest developments in steam technology. To this end it was decided to make some modifications to 30 locomotives of the latest batches of new 4-6-0s rolling off the production line at Crewe Works. Caprotti valve gear and Timken cannon type roller bearing axleboxes for the coupled wheels were the two major alterations being implemented. To ensure the best fit of these new components the relative sections of the standard Black 5 design had to be reconfigured to best accommodate this new type of valve gear and axlebox. In particular the trailing pair of driving wheels was moved back no less than 4ins. and the boiler centre line pitched 2ins. higher. These modifications generated an additional 2-3 tons in the overall weight of the locomotives. Six locomotives of the experimental batch were to be fitted with double chimneys and electric lighting whilst one locomotive, No. 4767, would have an experimental set of outside Stephenson motion to act as a comparison with Caprotti and Walschaerts types.

In summary the proposals were –

Nos.	Valve gear	Bearings
4738-47	Caprotti	Plain
4748-57	Caprotti	Timken roller
4758-66	Walschaerts	Timken roller
4767	Stephenson link	Timken roller

Eleven members of this elite group had been completed by the end of 1947 and the first two to emerge in 1948 were Nos. 4748 and 4749 which were completed by the third week in February 1948. Five more, Nos. 4750-54, were finished by the middle of April. The final 'guinea pig' to see the light of day was No. 4746 which was completed in August. Detailed running and maintenance costs would be maintained for these locomotives in service to enable comparisons to be made and upon which future design decisions would be based. A brief word on Arturo Caprotti, an Italian engineer (22

March 1881 – 9 February 1938) who invented the valve gear named after him in the early 1920s. This gear used poppet valves and camshafts instead of the more usual piston valves used in other types of valve gear. Basing his design on automotive valves, having worked for the Florentia car plant in Florence where he rose to become works director, he made several modifications in order to adapt the valves for steam locomotive use. He joined forces with Worcester based engineering company Heenan & Froude whom we have previously come across in connection with the provision of equipment for the Rugby Testing Station. His gear was first tested on an Italian State Railways mixed traffic locomotive in 1921 and although it proved to be more costly and complicated than standard piston valves, it did improve the locomotive's performance considerably and in the following years similar gears were fitted to over 300 Italian State Railways (FS) locomotives and over 70 narrow gauge locomotives. By the 1930s it had been fitted on some 334 FS locomotives and on 77 narrow-gauge locomotives.

The British experience of Caprotti valve gear began in 1926 when LMS No. 5908, one of the Claughton 4-6-0s, was so fitted. Following trials nine further examples were rebuilt with Caprotti gear and the conclusion was drawn that the Caprotti fitted

Plaque placed on Caprotti's birthplace in 1958 marking the 20th anniversary of his death. Licensed under Wikipedia Creative Commons licence.

locomotives were more economical on coal and water than similar Walschaerts fitted examples. However with an adjustment to the Walschaerts gear to stem leakage of steam past the valve heads, through the use of several narrow rather than one wide piston ring, it was found that Walschaerts proved to be just as economical as Caprotti but with considerably less costs associated with their fitting. The 10 Caprotti fitted Claughtons were all withdrawn in 1935/6 and no further LMS locomotives were fitted with the gear.

On the LNER two Class B3 4-6-0s were fitted with the gear in 1929 followed by a further pair in 1938/9. One of the first pair was rebuilt with Walschaerts gear in 1943 but the remaining trio ran with Caprotti gear until withdrawal in 1946/7. Thus when Ivatt undertook his trials on the Black 5s in 1948 he was dealing with something of a mixed bag of previous results

with Caprotti being considerably more expensive to manufacture and fit than its rivals but, as much of the mechanism was enclosed this did reap benefits in terms of less wear and tear during everyday running and did allow completely independent control of admission and exhaust which could lead to efficiencies of operation. The Black 5 conversions of 1948 were not to be the end of the Caprotti story on BR however as during the construction of the Standard classes during the 1950s Caprotti gear was once more tried on the solitary 8P pacific No. 71000 *Duke of Gloucester* and on 30 of the Class 5 4-6-0s, Nos. 73125 – 73154. The performance of No. 71000 in its BR days was rather lacklustre but much of this has subsequently been put down to design faults which have been rectified in preservation. No. 73129 is the sole example of the Caprotti fitted Standard Class 5s to survive in preservation.

Below: Close-up of the Caprotti piston & valve gear fitted to No. 44742. IMAGE SOURCE: REV79-A-1-6
Opposite Top: This view of Caprotti fitted No. 44738 was taken at Bangor. IMAGE SOURCE: FH190
Opposite Bottom: With British Railways on the tender but still carrying M4748 on the cabside, this Caprotti fitted Black Five is seen passing through Crewe. IMAGE SOURCE: GEO59

Last of the line

Replacement of motive power through age and obsolescence has been a feature of railways since the first locomotives were introduced and here we look at some examples of the last of their line which were withdrawn in 1948.

Above: LAST OF THE RAILMOTORS 10617
Railmotor No. 10617 is seen in LMS days in this undated view taken at what is believed to be Horwich. IMAGE SOURCE: NS204038

Built at Horwich and Newton Heath over a five year period from 1906 to a Hughes design, this class of 18 railmotors for the L&YR comprised an 0-4-0 locomotive attached to a trailer. Inherited by the LMS at the grouping and numbered 10600-17, the first withdrawals came in 1927 with only one remaining in service to be inherited by BR in 1948. This, No. 10617, often to be found on the shuttle service between Blackrod and Horwich, was itself withdrawn in March 1948.

Opposite top: LAST OF THE GLASGOW & SOUTH WESTERN LOCOMOTIVES
LMS ex-G&SWR 0-6-2T No.16911 is seen at Penrith in this undated view. IMAGE SOURCE: MP31101

Only one example of this ex-G&SWR 45 Class of 0-6-2T locomotive, No 16905 survived into BR ownership and this was promptly withdrawn without receiving its BR number. Four locomotives were sold into industrial service and the last survivor, the former LMS 16908, worked at Ashington Colliery until 1955.

Opposite bottom: LAST OF THE 'DUNALASTAIR III' CLASS 14434
LMS ex-CALEY 4-4-0 McIntosh 'Dunalastair III' Class No.14434 is seen at Dalry Road shed Edinburgh on 1 August 1937. IMAGE SOURCE: MP31296

The Caledonian Railway 721 Class, known as 'Dunalastair' was a class of 4-4-0s designed by McIntosh and introduced in 1896. All survived to be absorbed by the LMS in 1923 and a few lasted into BR days. Four different versions were developed including the 900 class known as 'Dunalastair IIIs' which were numbered 14337-14348, with those type IIIs rebuilt with superheaters numbered 14434-37. The final example, renumbered by BR to 54434 but never applied was based at Aviemore and withdrawn in April 1948.

L M S 16911

L M S 14434

WEST E

LAST OF THE 'GEORGE V' CLASS No. 25350

LMS 4-4-0 'George V' class No. 25350 is pictured in 1948 at Crewe South depot. It had originally been named *India*.
IMAGE SOURCE: NS203363

Ninety locomotives introduced during July 1910 by Bowen-Cooke were basically superheated versions of the Precursor class and all were originally named. Passing to the LMS, they were renumbered on two occasions and several names were removed to be applied to the new Jubilee class. Withdrawals began in 1935 and by the time of nationalisation just three remained operational with the final two, 25350 and 25373, both going in May 1948.

LAST OF THE ORIGINAL 'DUNALASTAIR IV' CLASS No. 14363

LMS 4-4-0 No. 14356 is on the turntable at Wemyss Bay on 12 July 1936.
IMAGE SOURCE: GB749

A total of 19 'Dunalastair IV' Class 140s were constructed between 1904-10 with two being rebuilt with superheaters in the period 1915-17. Three passed into BR ownership with the last of the original examples, No. 14363, being withdrawn in October 1948. One of the two rebuilt examples remarkably lasted in service until 1958.

LAST OF THE STEAM RAILCARS No. 29988

Moffat station sees the smoky departure of Caley/LMS railmotor No. 29988 in the mid-1940s.
IMAGE SOURCE: MC10028M

Introduced 1905 to a Whale design for the L&NWR, this 0-4-0T comprised a locomotive combined with a coach on a single underframe with the locomotive chimney protruding through the roof. Used latterly on the Beattock and Moffat branch services, No. 29988 was the last self propelled steam railcar to operate on BR and was withdrawn in November 1948. At one time there were over 200 such vehicles in service on Britain's railways.

LAST OF THE F7 TANKS 7093/4

F7 No. 7094 is parked out of use at Glasgow's Cowlairs Works in 1948, the final year of operation of these tank locomotives.
IMAGE SOURCE: NS205725

A surprisingly large number of locomotives of the 2-4-2T wheel arrangement were constructed for various UK railway companies including Sinclair's GER examples which eventually numbered 262, Webb's L&NWR classes totalling 380 examples and 330 for the L&YR. The last examples of Holden's small F7 class of 2-4-2Ts, Nos. 7093/7094, were withdrawn from service at the end of 1948. Introduced in 1909 to replace the 0-6-0Ts of the J65 class, they were never very successful and only 12 were constructed at Stratford Works for light passenger duties. Crews actually preferred the J65s and in view of their overly large cabs with enormous windows in relation to the overall size of the locomotives, they were christened 'Crystal Palace' tanks. Some examples were fitted with Westinghouse brake pumps for auto train working and could often be found in East Anglia working lightly loaded services to Ramsey, St. Ives, Aldeburgh and Maldon amongst other destinations. During the LNER era some migrated to Scotland as evidenced by the

Bottom left: A4 Pacific No. 60034 *Peregrine* was renamed *Lord Faringdon* in March in honour of Alexander Henderson 1st. Baron Faringdon (1850-1934) who had been a prolific financier of railways in both Great Britain and overseas before becoming chairman of the Great Central Railway (GCR) between 1899 – 1922 following which he became deputy chairman of its successor, the LNER, until his death. This A4 was not the first locomotive to have been named after him for in 1902 the GCR allocated the name *Sir Alexander* to No. 1014 of Class 11B, later LNER class D9, and in 1913 the first of the new Director Class locomotives No. 429 was named *Sir Alexander Henderson*. Upon his elevation to the peerage, rather than renaming No. 429, the nameplate was removed from this locomotive and instead a newly built 4-6-0 of LNER class B3 No. 6169 was named *Lord Faringdon* which it carried until withdrawal from service in December 1947. No. 60034 Lord Faringdon carried the name until withdrawal in 1966. IMAGE SOURCE: V388

Top left: LNER, formerly GCR, 4-6-0 of the Robinson B3 Class No.6169 *Lord Faringdon*, seen here at Nottingham Victoria, was the holder of the original name later awarded to A4 No. 60034. IMAGE SOURCE: MP40882

Bottom right: No. 60034 *Lord Faringdon* at Aberdeen. IMAGE SOURCE: SM295

Also, whilst we are on the subject of A4s, a plaque encircled with a laurel wreath and headed LNER has been fitted to 60022 *Mallard* recording the fact that "On 3rd July 1938 this locomotive attained a world speed record for steam traction of 126 miles per hour". The plaque has been mounted on the side of the boiler casing.

There has been a rapid name change for West Country pacific No. 34025 *Roughtor*, named for a few days in April 1948 after the second highest peak in Cornwall at 547m above sea level located on Dartmoor. It was renamed *Whimple* on 3 May 1948 after a village in east Devon on the main Salisbury – Exeter line noted for its cider producing apple orchards. *(Ed. Probably just as well that the Southern region did not in their wisdom choose to rename it after the highest peak on Bodmin Moor - 'Brown Willy' at 420m, which might well have caused some ribald amusement amongst enginemen and the travelling public. Why it was renamed so shortly after the original nameplate was affixed remains something of a mystery as all the pacifics in the group 34021-30 were named after west country localities rather than specific towns and indeed the first twenty West Countries were named after major towns and the most important holiday resorts in the SR area, so naming a locomotive after lowly Whimple, population of just 680 in 1901 which had risen to only 1,173 in 2011, was even more surprising. It may be of course, taking the cynical view, that some SR bigwig lived in the locality or perhaps lobbying from the cider industry, which generated much traffic for the railway, had something to do with it? If any reader has a plausible explanation I would be fascinated to hear it.)*

The Great Western coat of arms has been fixed to the splasher of the middle pair of driving wheels below the nameplate of Castle Class No. 7007 *Great Western* to commemorate the long history of the GWR. The coat of arms consists of a combination of the arms and crests of London and Bristol with the mottos 'Domine dirige nos' and 'Virtute et Industria', translating as 'Lord guide us' and 'Virtue or valour and industry'. The locomotive was originally named *Ogmore Castle* but when it was realised that it was the final express passenger locomotive to be constructed under GWR auspices before nationalisation, it was appropriately renamed in January 1948.

Brief encounters

This regular section will feature oddities and some of the more bizarre items of news...............

RAILWAY SUNDAY

The Daily Herald newspaper has started a campaign to celebrate the nationalisation of the railways on Sunday 4 January to be known as Railway Sunday. Apparently a Sunday was chosen to reduce interference with railway services. On that day the NUR held mass meetings at many railway centres with the London meeting held in the Coliseum theatre attended by more than 2,000 railwaymen. There is an unofficial suggestion that the first Sunday of every year be observed as 'Railway Sunday'. *(Ed: The Daily Herald, supported by the Labour party and published with their interests very much in mind, lasted until 1964 when it was re-launched as The Sun. Of Railway Sunday nothing more was heard.)*

SORRY MATE YOUR NAME'S TOO LONG!

The original nameplates fabricated for new A2 Class No. 525 were inscribed Arthur H. Peppercorn in line with the LNER's habit of rendering the first name and surname on the plates of people so honoured. However these nameplates proved to be just too long when they came to be affixed to the smoke deflectors of the pacific. Consequently new plates were made with the shortened version reading *A. H. Peppercorn.* Did they consider just dropping the middle initial and going with 'Arthur Peppercorn' although Ivatt also received similar rather formal treatment with H.A. Ivatt on No. 60123 as did *W.P. Allen* on No. 60114. Looking at photographs of No. 525 however

reveals that even A.H. Peppercorn covered the whole width of the smoke deflector. *(Ed: I wonder what happened to the original plates for No. 525 – if they were not scrapped or melted down they would be worth a fortune today on the railwayana market no doubt.)*

TAMWORTH TROUBLEMAKERS

Following interference with lineside equipment and instances of trespassing, a 'spotting ban' has been imposed at Tamworth station in Staffordshire where enthusiasts are wont to gather at this prime vantage point where traffic on the low level main line to Euston and on the high level Derby to Birmingham line can be simultaneously observed. Described as 'normally the most decorous of people', the reputation of true railway enthusiasts

in the area has been tarnished by the misdeeds of a 'small minority of irresponsible youngsters whose interest in trains is likely to be ephemeral'. At present the ban only applies to Tamworth and the London Midland region has indicated that it does not intend to extend it to other locations unless similar difficulties occur. *(Ed: BR did from time to time target trainspotters at its stations and other premises and I recall a notice at Nine Elms depot in the 1960s that read 'Train Spotters are prohibited from entering this yard'. Also in steam days staff at Wigan North Western station, who were generally tolerant of spotters, did on occasion if numbers got too great, resort to a tannoy broadcast stating 'It is now time for all trainspotters to leave the station!'.)* This became something of a perennial problem and five years later in 1953 a poster would be produced by BR headed 'To Loco Spotters' which went on to state 'British Railways welcome your interest and enthusiasm for railway matters'. Somewhat more anthropomorphically it also went on to elaborate that 'Our engines are proud to have their speeds, numbers and wheel arrangements recorded in your books.' But here comes the rub: 'You have heard of the Highway Code – here is our Spotters' Code.' There followed a list of four basic rules including the exhortation 'Don't jump on parcels or mailbags – there may be a present for you inside'. The poster ended with the warning that 'If you take risks or misbehave you will not be allowed on the platforms – not just you but all your pals as well!'

FEMINISTS HAVE THE UPPER HAND

Apparently complaints have been received by BR about the clarity of some railway station announcers. Some male voices have been criticised for being 'too rasping' and it is claimed that the voice of your average untrained man becomes far too harsh and blurred when amplified by microphone and (horror of horrors!) some local dialects render announcements practically unintelligible to strangers to the area. It is a pleasure to hear most female announcers speak (hopefully in the Received Pronunciation manner of Celia Johnson for example) for announcing is an art and candidates require careful selection and training. Also of importance of course is the quality of the loud speakers, many of which leave a great deal to be desired especially in the echoing surroundings of large cavernous stations.

GOING DOWN – BASEMENT FLOOR

On 13 April, M7 0-4-4T No. 672 disgraced itself at Waterloo. As four coal wagons were being propelled onto the hydraulic lift that services the subterranean Waterloo & City Line, by which rolling stock from the underground railway could be raised to the level of the main line for repairs, the lift platform tilted following a failure to engage the required supports correctly. Two wagons had already been placed on the lift when it started to sink and it carried the other wagons and locomotive with it, the whole lot plunging down the 42 foot lift shaft with the Drummond tank coming to rest upside down with its wheels in the air atop the wagons. Services on the Waterloo & City Line had to be suspended as the fire in the locomotive continued to burn until all the coal had been consumed. In view of the fact that there was no practicable method of retrieving any of the rolling stock, the decision was taken that both the locomotive and wagons should be cut up in situ and parts from the M7 were subsequently sent to Eastleigh Works and used as spares for other members of the class. Fortunately Driver A. Wheeler and Fireman A. W. Sutton jumped off the locomotive just in time and staff working at the bottom of the shaft also escaped injury. A company photographer who recorded the incident on film was ordered to destroy the negative to prevent embarrassing publicity for the newly formed Southern region but seemingly this was not done as a view of the stricken locomotive can be found on the internet. *(Ed: Just type in 'M7 liftshaft Waterloo 1948' and you should be able to find it.)* No. 672 thus became only the second member of the M7 class to be withdrawn, the experimentally boilered No. 126 having been taken out of service as non standard in 1937.

Like a beetle on its back with its legs in the air, M7 No. 672, which had plunged down the lift shaft at Waterloo, reveals the scale of the problem facing engineers attempting to rescue the locomotive. IMAGE SOURCE: MARYEVANS.COM

Accident report

The sheer volume of accidents in 1948 is perhaps surprising in today's health and safety conscious climate but many of them were of a relatively minor nature and only the most serious involved an official investigation and subsequent publication of a written report. The table below records all 26 accidents that occurred on the newly formed BR in 1948 together with brief details of causes, results and casualties. With 60 fatalities and 283 serious injuries in just one year, the table makes sombre reading. The official reports often took some time to compile and did not appear until the following year. They included recommendations to improve safety and hopefully prevent recurrences. By way of comparison, in the period 2000-2021 there have been fewer fatalities than in the one year of 1948, the figure for this 22 year period being 50 which gives an average of just 2.27 per year.

Date	Location	Causes	Result	Casualties		Report
				Fatalities	Injured	
23 Jan	London Bridge	Driver error	SPAD head on collision	3	79	YES
11 Feb	Crayford	Rear collision		0	0	
1 Mar	Dewsbury Moor	Road vehicle driver error	Collision	1	0	
1 Mar	Connington North	Road vehicle driver error, fog	Collision	6	5	YES
7 Mar	Lamington	Inadequate maintenance, Inoperative equipment, boiler water shortage	Firebox failure	1	1	YES
10 Mar	S/ Bermondsey Junc.	Collision with structure	Derailment	0	0	
17 Apr	Winsford	Signalman error	Derailment telescoping	24	30	YES
12 May	Heaton Lodge	Rear collision		0	0	
18 May	Wath Road Junction	Inadequate maintenance & inspection	Derailment	8	56	YES
17 Jul	New Southgate	Track defect	Derailment train split	1	11	YES
17 Jul	Ardler Junction	Driver/signalman error, SPAD	Derailment	2	12	YES
21 Aug	Hatfield-St. Albans	Insecure points, vandalism	Buffer stop collision	0	0	
23 Aug	Scarborough	Head on collision	Derailment	0	9	
15 Sep	Garton	Road vehicle collision	Fire	3	6	YES
15 Sep	Codnor Park-Langley Mill	Bearing failure	Boiler water shortage	0	2	YES
24 Sep	Glasgow Charing Cross	Rear collision		0	11	
7 Oct	Northwich	Head on collision	Derailment	1	1	
16 Oct	Connington North	Road vehicle driver error	Collision **	1	0	YES
28 Oct	Neath	Rear collision		0	4	
12 Nov	New Mills	Fog	Rear collision	0	2	
18 Nov	Woolwich Arsenal	Driver, signalman and guard error, SPAD	Rear collision	2	16	YES
23 Nov	Bainton level crossing	Crossing keeper error	Vehicle collision	1	0	YES
29 Nov	Griseburn	Guard error, failure to secure brakes	Runaway train collision with structure	1	2	YES
30 Nov	Stockport	Driver error, fog, SPAD	Rear collision	5	36	YES
30 Nov	Clapham Junction	Fog, rear collision	Fire	0	0	
7 Dec	Cowden-Hever	Defective boiler	Firebox failure	0	0	YES
16 Dec	***					
Total				**60**	**283**	

SPAD   Signal passed at danger
**   The former Mayor of Peterborough Arthur Mellows, and his dog, were killed in their car.
***   The 'Western Daily Press' recorded the death of a railway employee at Mangotsfield struck by a mail train on 16 December although this accident does not appear to have entered official records.

First of the many - the main line diesel twins

The first of the pair of 1,600hp diesel electric main line locomotives, No. 10000, designed by Ivatt and built in six months at Derby, appeared in December 1947 followed by its twin, No. 10001, in July 1948. A joint venture between English Electric and BR, they were the first of their fleet of main line diesel locomotives and were to be the proving ground for many aspects of diesel operations. The LMS, who had steered the project, were keen to see their insignia rather than that of BR on the side of the locomotive and it was presented to the public at Euston on 18 December just a few days before nationalisation. After proving trials between St. Pancras, Derby and Manchester, which began in the middle of January with a 12 coach train of 393 tons tare weight, No. 10000 entered traffic in February operating a twice daily London – Derby return schedule. From 6 April the new diesel was making two round trip journeys a day

between London and Derby with a rostered mileage of 3,100/week. It was joined by its twin, No. 10001, in July and they often worked in tandem as at only 1,600hp each they were unsuited to solo hauling of the fastest and heaviest express services. Their regular workings as a pair commenced on 5 October handling Euston – Glasgow services. Apparently Ivatt sat on the correspondence from BR requiring that the LMS logo on No. 10000 should be replaced by the BR one until his retirement in 1951. A bay in the paint shop at Derby, set aside to act as a maintenance and repair depot for diesel locomotives, was partitioned off and two 50 ton cranes spanning three tracks dedicated to the diesels.

They had 16 cylinders and the engine, main and auxiliary generators formed one unit which was mounted on three point bearings resting on rubber

Operating a St. Pancras – Derby service, No. 10000 is seen at Sheet Stores Junction near Trent recorded very precisely by the photographer as 4:44pm on 29 March 1948. **Image Source: C4/1**

10000 is captured at Luton in 1948 proudly displaying its LMS credentials. IMAGE SOURCE: JOHN BATTS 008-2

pads to reduce vibration. The chassis was carried on two six wheeled bogies each with three traction motors. The finished product weighed in at a massive 121 ½ tons and could carry 900 gallons of fuel oil, 595 gallons of water and 131 gallons of oil for the train heating boiler. Each of the six axles had its own traction motor and could deliver a tractive effort of 41,400 lbs. on starting and for short periods ascending gradients. Drivers and firemen had adjustable cushioned seats and electric heaters in the cabs which, according to the commentator of the film mentioned below, 'made driving 10000 almost an armchair job'. Cabs were of course provided at each end thus removing the need for reversing the locomotive. A

film produced by the Advertising & Publicity Dept. at Euston entitled 'Main Line Diesel' can be viewed on Youtube detailing the construction of the locomotive. It also includes a section on the new Stanier pacific No. 6256 against which 10000 would be pitted in comparative trials. They were both exhibited at Euston on 17 December 1947 in the presence of Ivatt and the General Managers of the LMS and of the English Electric companies. *(Ed: Both diesel locomotives were subsequently allocated to Willesden depot with No. 10000 being withdrawn in 1963 and No. 10001 following in 1968 but today the Ivatt Diesel Re-creation Society has plans to construct a replica of No. 10000.)*

NEW MIDLAND TANKS TRIALLED IN THE SOUTH
No. 42198, built at Derby, is seen on Southern region metals at Tonbridge. IMAGE SOURCE: MC30195

Above: Trials involving Nos. 42198 and 42199 began on 19 April with specials being worked from Waterloo-Basingstoke and from Victoria to Tunbridge Wells West. Workings were then arranged on ordinary services based on Nine Elms, Stewarts Lane, Bricklayers Arms, Ashford, Tunbridge Wells and Dover sheds with particular attention paid to the Oxted lines of the Central Section. Whilst running a special from Victoria – Ashford, No. 42199 was observed bunker first topping 80mph. At the conclusion of the trials they were transferred to Stirling in Scotland where they arrived on 29 June. Quite why they were tested on the SR is unclear.

THIRD MEMBER OF THE CO-CO TRIO ARRIVES
This view of the newly out-shopped electric locomotive No. 20003 with a test train is believed to have been taken at Selhurst.
IMAGE SOURCE: ARTHUR TAYLOR

Opposite top: Construction of the third member of the trio was well advanced by the time of nationalisation and on 22 August 1948 it was towed from Eastleigh to Durnsford Road, Wimbledon by N class No. 31827 ready for testing to commence the following week. It was anticipated that it would be ready for traffic at the end of October but this was delayed and it was noted at Brighton under repair on 9 October. It did not finally come into service, on a freight duty, until 10 November. It featured a more austere SUB type EMU cab front differing from the HAL type of the two earlier models CC1 and CC2 and it was finished in SR malachite green with white lining. The British Railways lettering 9 ins. high was rendered in yellow and black on the bodyside.

YANKEE TANKS TAKE 'OVER HERE'

Opposite bottom: Popularised by the comedian Tommy Trinder, the phrase 'Overpaid, overfed, oversexed and over here' was applied to American GIs in Britain during World War 2. Yankee tank No. s73, now lettered British Railways, is seen at work in Southampton Docks where this class of 0-6-0T took 'over here' from the 0-4-0 B4 tanks. At the end of August 1948 only four Class B4s remained in the docks - Nos. 81 and 85, which were stored in the old Docks shed and Nos. 97 and 147, stored in an old fruit warehouse near the Ocean Dock coaling stage in the old Docks. Goods shunting was now monopolised by the USA tanks and the following carried British Railways lettering - Nos. S64, S73, 30066, 30067 and 30072. Of these, No. 30072 had Gill Sans lettering and a smoke-box numberplate fitted. IMAGE SOURCE: S C TOWNROE

Loss Leader?
by Kevin Robertson

At the time of nationalisation the 'big four' already had their respective planned locomotive building programmes mapped out. So far as the Southern region was concerned this was mainly 'more of the same', meaning further batches of Pacific types, both 'Merchant Navy' and 'West Country / Battle of Britain' engines. Elsewhere Swindon were constructing 'Castle' class engines and the Eastern busying themselves with their own 'Pacific' types, all traditional – do we really say that concerning a Bulleid 'Pacific' – but traditional in so far as they were 'conventional designs', each of course to the whims of the particular former company.

Rumbling in the background however, was one steam design that was vastly different from any other and with its origins strangely on that most electric of railways, the Southern. That design was of course what we now know to be the 'Leader' and whilst it would not actually turn a wheel until 1949, a brief update on development and with it progress in 1948 may not come amiss.

Without wishing to teach the reader to 'suck eggs', suffice to say the design of this 'tank engine' – we should really call it a tank engine as both boiler / bunker / and water tank were mounted on the same frame – had been started back in 1944, when 25 engines of an unspecified type were approved by the SR Board. Approval for construction of engines to an unspecified design might appear strange and indeed it was, for what followed was a succession of false starts varying from tank engines to short bogie steam engines and beyond. The beyond was what grew into Leader, in short a design where the no doubt genuine beliefs of the designer Oliver Bulleid knew no bounds and extreme concept followed on from extreme concept, so that by 1948 the stage was set for a double bogie steam engine far different from what perhaps the traffic department had originally wanted; which was in reality a modern and versatile large tank engine.

We should break off slightly at this point to discuss the large tank engine concept. Recall too that the Sevenoaks disaster of 1927 was still fresh in the minds of several senior Southern officers and despite already having various large tank engines at their disposal, the former LBSCR 'Baltic' Tank engines, I1X , I2, and I3 classes, LSWR 'G16', and SECR 'J' class, plus the Maunsell 'W' design, none of these were being used to any effect on major

Eastleigh works, 25 August 1948. Leader boiler and firebox crown, the latter supported by four thermic syphons. Five boilers would be built, all steam tested but without any riveting along the joints. The design of the engine had the boiler offset by nine inches from the centre line. This allowed space for a narrow 'communication' corridor between the fireman's position and the driving cabs at either end. The firehole was similarly offset to the left of the rear firebox plate and hardly ideal for placing coal on the right hand side of the firebox. The fireman of necessity worked in a depression in the footplate, giving him headroom at least but little escape from the enormous heat that developed within his closed compartment.
IMAGE SOURCE: REG CURL

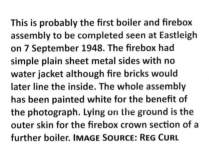

This is probably the first boiler and firebox assembly to be completed seen at Eastleigh on 7 September 1948. The firebox had simple plain sheet metal sides with no water jacket although fire bricks would later line the inside. The whole assembly has been painted white for the benefit of the photograph. Lying on the ground is the outer skin for the firebox crown section of a further boiler. IMAGE SOURCE: REG CURL

passenger work; the 'W' in particular being officially barred from passenger duties other than working occasional empty carriage stock (ECS) trains. Bulleid felt his 'tank engine' would be better than all of these, and in particular more versatile in its capacities. In short all the advantages of a tank engine but with greater power.

At this point the reader, knowing as we expect nearly all already do, the eventual outcome of Leader, could well ask, "Why did someone not stop or at least constrain Bulleid?". The answer was simple. The work environment was very different in the late 1940s compared to today. Back at that time one questioned one's superior at the potential peril of your own career. The gap between the lowly office boy and the chief draughtsman might have seemed great, but it was still nothing compared with that between the chief draughtsman and the CME. Many saw Bulleid as simply being 'rather clever'. His Pacific designs might not have been perfect, but what they had done was bring the Southern Railway steam stock back on to the map - modern designs yes with radical features but were they not galloping away everywhere and similarly loved by many, although perhaps not by the fitters. In consequence his staff did not only do as they were bidden but did so in the genuine belief that it would work. It was only later as the concept began to fall apart that some too began to

doubt the wisdom of the chief and began to pull back.

With a Labour government now in power it was only going to be a matter of time before the railways were nationalised and consequently it was a race to present the new order, British Railways, with a project if not complete, at least far enough advanced so that it might be permitted to continue. We may suspect also Bulleid was using his guile to the effect that it would be a little while before external pressure was brought to bear and he therefore had some time available to him. Even so for such a radical design much time was needed for everything was new. It was also not as if existing components might be used; indeed apart, literally, from the buffers, couplings, and whistles – recall there were two, one at each end – everything else ended up being made from scratch.

Hence 1947 was spent completing – and then changing the detail design, then changing it again, and finally perhaps back to what it had been originally, all this before it was possible to order parts and then being compelled to wait upon their manufacture. Major components were made at both Ashford, main frames and bogie frames, and Eastleigh, boilers and wheels. Brighton, where final assembly would take place, may well have been similarly involved as we have no information as to where the cylinder castings were produced.

Progress is now apparent in this view taken in about October 1948 with the boiler and bunker in position showing its corridor side. The smokebox has also been added showing the flat top where the vacuum reservoirs will be placed. On the extreme left is an incomplete bogie. Note too the 'Idaglas' insulation that has been partly applied to the boiler whilst the rectangular 'box' alongside the firebox is a new addition compared to the original design and was referred to as the 'mantle tank'. This provided additional water capacity that was intended to shield the inside of the locomotive slightly from the searing heat of the firebox sides. In practice it acted as little more than a 'radiator' with the water within heated by conduction from the firebox on one side. It was similarly not particularly effective in providing extra water capacity for, aside from restricting the corridor space further, the feed water within was heated which rendered the injectors less effective.
IMAGE SOURCE: DON BROUGHTON COLLECTION

Consequently at the start of 1948 it would be fair to say that no physical work had yet commenced but by the end of the same year, the main frames were set up at Brighton Works and at least some of the boilers had been delivered to Sussex. It must also be mentioned that whilst five engines had been authorised an order for a further 31 placed by the Southern Railway "straight off the drawing board" on the eve of Nationalisation was fortunately never confirmed by BR. Work was concentrated upon getting a single engine completed as rapidly as possible for the reasons previously stated. In addition, during 1948 lessons, and not always very good lessons, were being learned from the running trials of No. 2039 *Hartland Point* (see page 30). Whilst it was no doubt intended to incorporate such lessons involving the use of sleeve valves into the Leader design, in reality this proved impossible without a major redesign which would have probably put the project back at least a further year. In the opinion of the present writer this may well have also resulted in its cancellation. Indeed the three salient points where the Leader design was so radically different were: the offset boiler with its dry-back firebox, the concept of a steam engine on two power bogies with the final drive achieved by chains, and the use of sleeve valves. In theory all promised advantages, it would not be until the first engine began trials before it was discovered whether all three produced the promised advantages.

The last named aspect certainly did not get off to a good start with No. 2039. As these were the main design differences from a conventional steam locomotive, the reader may quickly see how to alter something in 1948 would thus have been difficult if not impossible.

Leader in 1948 then was little more than a kit of parts - and with some bits missing. We know that by 11 May 1948 the main frames for at least one engine were in position within the Erecting Shop at Brighton Works together with one and possibly two bogie frames. By the end of 1948 at least one set of main frames had been erected with the boiler and firebox assembly added and the bunker in position. Some wheels and axle sets had also arrived but other major work remained to be done; we have for example no information as to where the final drive chains were manufactured most likely an outside source. It would be a further six months beyond the end of 1948 before everything was finally ready and what was then identified as BR No. 36001 would steam for the first time – and then the fun would really begin. *(Ed: The press would go on to have a field day over the costs of this project to the taxpayer, reported as £178,000, £6.5m in today's money, in 1951 when the project was aborted but which was subsequently reported as £500,000, £18.2m today, when the press in the form of the Sunday Despatch featured the story in 1953.)*

Also making the news

New Thurgoland tunnel on Sheffield - Wath electrification scheme completed in October.

The 1½ mile Polhill tunnel on SR route between Knockholt and Dunton Green on the Charing Cross - Tonbridge line closed for relaying, reballasting and provision of improved drainage.

British and French delegates meet to discuss the Channel tunnel.

Three 4-4-2T Tilbury tanks transferred to Dundee.

Appeal begins to save Stephenson's cottage at Wylam.

Former LNER line from Newbury Park and Hainault reopened after electrification on 31 May by London Transport. This line is now part of the Central line.

The end of the streamliners announced with the disbanding of former LNER streamline sets which are to be used as ordinary stock in a number of express trains.

All Class A4 had their garter blue with crimson wheels pre-war livery restored.

BR catering now the responsibility of the Hotels Executive which take over hotel, refreshment room and restaurant car operation.

Waterloo station centenary exhibition with Adams T3 4-4-0 No 563, Terrier 0-6-0T *Boxhill* and West Country pacific No. 34017 *Ilfracombe* on display.

New buffet lounge cars for the 'Flying Scotsman' service.

Hadrian Bar introduced on the 'Tees Tyne Pullman' service with panelling, bar and table tops in the new wonder material 'Formica' which is stain resistant and cigarette proof.

New BR posters unveiled featuring Terence Cuneo image of the Royal Border bridge and Southern 'See the West Country from the train' featuring Little Petherick Creek bridge near Padstow by Eric Hesketh.

Second public open day at Longmoor military railway held on 15 September.

Eight previously unnamed 'Patriots' to receive names from former LNWR locomotives.

1947 Winsford accident report published.

550 stations have entered the 'Best Kept Station' award.

Five former LMS 3F tank locomotives, to become BR Nos. 47589/47607/47611/47659/47660, have been repatriated from France via Dover and taken to Derby works for reconditioning.

No. 7511, the last of the former Metropolitan railway H class 4-4-4Ts condemned.

IN THE NEXT ISSUE OF RAILWAY TIMES COVERING BRITISH RAILWAYS IN 1949

Amongst other items it is hoped to feature the following –

DOUBLE DECKER EMU
NEW NAMED EXPRESSES
ALL STEEL COACHES
TAVERN CARS
RETIREMENT OF CMEs; BULLEID, HAWKSWORTH AND PEPPERCORN
NEW WESTERN REGION 1500 CLASS PANNIER TANKS
LIVERPOOL STREET - SHENFIELD ELECTRIFICATION
THE BR CONSTRUCTION PROGRAMME
SELF-WEIGHING TENDERS

Also in the next issue we will cover the trial of Beyer-Garratt No. 69999 at Bromsgrove for banking duties on the Lickey incline. *FH337*